THE SECRETS OF SUCCESSFUL SELLING HABITS

THE SECRETS
OF SUCCESSFUL
SELLING
HABITS

Zig Ziglar

FOREWORD BY
TOM ZIGLAR

&

MEDIA

MEDIA

Published 2019 by Gildan Media LLC
aka G&D Media
www.GandDmedia.com

FIRST EDITION 2019

Front Cover design by David Rheinhardt of Pyrographx

Design by Meghan Day Healey of Story Horse, LLC

Library of Congress Cataloging-in-Publication Data is available upon request

ISBN: 978-1-7225-0121-1

10   9   8   7   6   5   4   3   2   1

Contents

Foreword

by Tom Ziglar

I'm excited that you are about to embark on journey of going through *The Secrets of Successful Selling*, by my father, Zig Ziglar.

We've brought this classic information back to you because we believe that the foundation stones of selling have not changed at all. Yes, our culture's changed, and the technology's changed, and way we do business has changed, but when you talk about a value proposition, when you talk about how people trust each other and what they expect, and when salespeople have a higher level of responsibility for integrity and morality than ever before, you're going to discover that this course is perfectly suited for what you do today.

I love *The Secrets of Successful Selling* because salespeople have an enormous responsibility, and opportunity, to help their customers and their prospects forgo future pain. What do I mean by *forgoing future pain?* I learned from one of my mentors, Rabbi Daniel Lapin, that in sales what we really want to do is we want to look into the future of our customer's life, and we want to picture that life.

We can picture that life *with* our product or service or *without* our product or service. When we understand that our product or service can help them overcome a problem before they even have it, then, I believe, we have a moral responsibility to offer them that product or service.

Yes, this is a far cry from what we see all the time on the Internet, which gives huge promises and doesn't really deliver anything of value. We have a huge moral responsibility to do what's right for our customer and our prospect. *The Secrets of Successful Selling* is based on that foundational belief.

In order to live out this moral responsibility to its fullest, we have to be professional. We have to have the technical skills. We have to know the right questions to ask. We have to take our own career seriously because until we do that, we're not servicing our customers the way we should. We're not helping our prospects understand the benefits of what we have to offer. A lot more is at stake than just a sale. It's dreams, really.

Here's the reality. When we do what we are equipped to do, when we have the gifts that we have been given and we use them to our fullest ability and in the right moral framework, then we solve more problems that are out there. When we solve more problems, we are rewarded.

Yes, that's a huge blessing to us, but it goes even one step further: our customers have dreams as well. Isn't it funny that the more we help others achieve their dreams, the more likely it is that we're going to achieve ours? It really does go back to my father's greatest quote of all: "You can have everything in life you want if you'll just help enough other people get what they want."

When we sell the right way with the right intention, and we bring a product or service that offers value, we're helping whomever we serve them to get closer to their dream, because that equips them to do what they do better. They solve problems in a better way, and they are rewarded for that.

We all know that dreams take time and money, so when people are solving problems and helping others achieve their dreams, that's when we solve our own. That's when we achieve our own dreams.

Tom Ziglar is the president of Ziglar Training Corporation, the author of *Live to Win*, and a successful platform speaker in his own right.

CHAPTER 1

Twenty-Five Things Every Salesperson Needs to Know

Zig

I've been in your sales shoes. I know what it is to absolutely have to make a sale today so you can put some gasoline in that automobile or some food on that table. *The Secrets of Successful Selling* is designed to help you sell today, but, far more importantly, it's designed to help you make the sale today in such a way that you can sell the same people tomorrow or next month or next year.

In my sales career, I've been in some homes where I could literally look through the floor and see the ground underneath. I've been in areas where I could look through the roof and see the skies up above. On occasion I've even been asked to leave. On the other side of the coin, I've taken the company's largest order. I've felt rejection in my sales career, and I've felt complete exhilaration.

The concepts I'll share with you come from nearly forty years of selling and observing the great ones, the truly successful sales professionals. In this segment, I will share what makes up the heart of your sales career, the five reasons people don't buy from you, and many reasons they *will* buy from you. I'll share more than thirty-nine professional sales skills and what I consider to be the most important part of the sales process.

In November 1975, I was in the market for a new automobile. I'd looked at a couple of Cadillacs and really fell in love with them. I thought that '76 model was sharp. I was told a good buddy of mine that I was looking at Cadillacs, and he said, "Until you've talked with Chuck Bellows over at Roger Meier, you're behind the times. Go see him. He'll really treat you right."

"You call him," I said, "and I'll be on my way over there while you're talking to him." He said, "Consider it done."

When I pulled into the parking spot, there really was only one spot left in that lot. There stood old Chuck. Even though I did not know him, I knew it was him because of his appearance, the way he was dressed, and the description I'd had. Very conservative, neatly attired. As I pulled in, Chuck opened the door for me. As he did, he said, "You have to be Zig Ziglar." I said, "Yes, I am."

Well, he's a very formal guy, so he said, "Well, Mr. Ziglar, let me tell you how glad I am to meet you, and I want to also say before I say anything else, this is truly a beautiful automobile you're driving." It really was. It was a Regency Oldsmobile, fully loaded, chocolate brown, and was in great condition. So he was paying me a sincere compliment.

That's the first sales point I would like to make in this presentation. A sincere compliment is a good way to start a presentation. The obvious key is *sincere*. If I'd been driving a dog and he'd said something like that, I'd have grabbed my pocketbook and run. But here's the second sales point: the best way to make a new sale is to make that prospect feel good about a previous purchase.

Some salespeople have made you feel so dumb for ever buying that piece of junk you want to swap that you are amazed that they're in business. As a young man, I shall never forget that my first brand-new car was an old Hudson automobile. I was so proud of that car that I made a special trip to Yazoo City, Mississippi, where I was raised, just to drive down Main Street. I really did.

Yet when it came time to swap that car in, the ugly things the salespeople said about it turned me off completely. The best way to make a new sale is to make that prospect feel good about the previous purchase.

Old Chuck said to me, "Zig, do you mind telling me where you got this car?" I said, "As a matter of fact, my neighbor across the street is an executive with General Motors, and he made arrangements for me to get a car through one of their dealers."

"Did you by any chance get one of the executive cars?" he asked. Here's sales point number three. A sales professional, if he really wants to be successful, will ask an awful lot of questions. That's the way you get information from people: ask them questions. When he asked me if I'd gotten one of the executive cars from the dealership, I said, "As a matter of fact, I did."

He smiled a little and said, "I'll bet you got a good deal, didn't you?" Well, I don't know how you are, but when somebody asks me if I made a good deal four years ago and implied that I did, I'm pleased. I modestly admitted—now remember this was back in 1975—I said, "Yes, Chuck. This car sold for $7600 when it was new. It only had 2100 miles on it, and I got it for $5600."

Old Chuck looked at me and said with sincere enthusiasm, "Man, you did get a good deal on that car."

I'll tell you what else I did. I just loaded the first barrel of his sales shotgun, and that brings us to sales point number four. They will give you pertinent information if you just ask. All you have to do is ask, and in most cases they will.

Chuck walked around the car a time or two and said, "It's absolutely gorgeous. Let me get the appraiser, and we'll go give it a look. I'm going to tell you one thing, Mr. Ziglar. If this car of yours is as nice on the inside as it is on the outside, we're going to be able to swap and make you happy, because we have such a beautiful inventory."

They got the appraiser, who went wherever it is they go when they do whatever it is they do looking cars over. I stood around there, waiting for them to come back, and I want to emphasize that the optimism that Chuck displayed really represents point number five: salespeople should be optimistic.

He had reason to be. He'd already said my car was nice. He had a beautiful inventory to work from, and he was giving me hope. That's what I want. He was giving me hope that we were going to be able to make a trade.

When they returned, I could see Chuck with a big smile on his face. I thought to myself, "Hey, he really likes my car." Then I have to confess to you. A thought ran through my mind. I didn't let it stay long, but it entered my mind that since he liked my car so much, I was going to be able to steal this deal. I even got to thinking maybe he was even going to pay me to swap, since he loved my car as much as he did.

Let me emphasize a point. I'm thinking like a buyer. That's what I'm supposed to do, because I'm buying, but sales point number six is this. To succeed in selling, you, the salesperson, must sit on both sides of the table. You have to think as a buyer, and you also have to think as a seller.

When Chuck stepped out of that car, he was grinning so wide, he could have eaten a banana sideways. I've never seen anything quite like it. I don't believe Chuck has ever been to drama school, but you're talking about a little display that he put on for me there. It was absolutely beautiful. It was amazing.

He stepped out of that car, and he closed the door. Then, like he couldn't believe it, he opened that door, and closed it again, and he was shaking his head. He said, "You know, Mr. Ziglar, this car of yours is even nicer on the inside than it is on the outside. I'm delighted you're here, but I'm a little puzzled. Why would you want to trade this gorgeous automobile in right now?"

Now that's powerful and it's positive. Some of you might think, "Why would he bring up something like that at this point? You're in there, you want to trade. What business is it of his? What difference does it make to him why you want to swap now?"

I say that's one of the strongest points in this entire presentation. Here's sales point number seven. If there's anything wrong, if there are any questions, if there are any objections, it is better to deal with them early in the presentation instead of later on as a rebuttal. This way you can sell on the offense and not on the defense. "Why do you want to swap right now?"

I smiled and said, "Well, Chuck, we have a family reunion on over in Mississippi, and I just think it'd kind of be nice to drive this new Cadillac over there."

Old Chuck thought that'd be nice too. As a matter of fact, I just loaded the second barrel of his sales shotgun. At that point, Chuck got out what I call his talking pad. That's what all professional salespeople must have. It doesn't necessarily have to be a big one, but he needs a talking pad so that when he's talking, he can also be figuring.

The reason is very simple. In our society, we have been conditioned to believe what we see and to doubt what we hear. All of our lives, we have heard this statement, "Now you can't believe everything you hear," but all of our lives we also have heard, "Listen, I saw it with my own two eyes, and seeing is believing."

Sales point number eight is that the prospect buys only when he believes and/or understands. When you write it out, his chance of believing and understanding is much greater.

Here's a very significant point. Chuck is selling me both logically and emotionally. See, if you use all logic in a presentation, then you'll have the best-educated prospect in town, and he'll go down the street to buy something. If you use all emotion in the presentation, then he'll get emotionally involved and buy, but then he might cancel on you the next day or the next week.

Tie them together, and he will buy logically today, or will buy emotionally today but based on some logical reasons, and consequently he will be sold. You're building a career. The logic are the eyes. We believe what we see. The emotion is the voice. We are moved by the tone and words in that voice.

Chuck got his pad out, and he starting figuring. As he started to figure, that big, beautiful smile was there, but I obviously was watching him carefully, because I was involved in this pretty deeply. After he'd been figuring a minute, that smile started to disappear, and as I watched that smile disappear my heart starting to sink a little bit.

I thought, "Oh, no. He's finding something, and I'm not going to be able to get that beautiful automobile."

He kept figuring, and that bland, neutral expression actually went into ugly. As a matter of fact, I have never seen such a high concentration of ugly in one spot in my lifetime as old Chuck was displaying right there.

As my heart started to sink, I just stood there not knowing what to do, but I give old Chuck Bellows credit for one thing. That guy is a fighter. I mean, he stayed right in there and figured and figured and figured, and pretty soon that ugly started to disappear, and it started moving back into neutral, and I caught myself pulling for him. "Hang in there, Chuck. Stay with it, boy. Stay with it. Stay with it."

Chuck hung in there all the way. Finally, he looked up at me with a big smile on his face, and using the pad, he said to me, "Mr. Ziglar, the good news to you is this. Because of our wonderful inventory, and because of the marvelous condition of your automobile, we're going to be able to swap with you for just $7385."

When he said that, I screamed like a stuck pig. I said, "Whoo, Chuck, man, that's a lot of money."

I almost had a heart attack when he said it. Don't misunderstand. I'm educated. I'd been reading the newspapers and seeing the TV ads. I knew the price of cars had gone up. My friends and my relatives had been telling me about it, but they were talking about something else. They were talking about *their* cars and their money. Old Chuck's talking to me about *my* car and *my* money.

When he started talking there about $7385—and that's not the way Chuck said it; he said, "$73-85," like the professional is supposed to—but when he said that with the right voice inflection, after I had screamed, he looked at me and half smiled and said, "Mr. Ziglar, is it too much?"

Now what is he saying to me? "Ziglar, if that's out of your price range, look, friend, if you can't handle that kind of money, be a man about it. Admit it. Just say you can't cut it." Do you think for one moment I would ever admit to a thing like that? There ain't no way.

But,sales point number nine is, when you use the right voice inflection—which later on we will teach you exactly how to do—I, the customer, have to make an important couple of decisions. Is he asking me if it's out of my range? That's one thing. Or, is he asking me, "Mr. Ziglar, as a wise and prudent businessman, is this $73-85 more than you're willing to pay?"

As a wise and prudent businessman, I plead guilty to that last one. You bet. So I said, "Chuck, that's simply more money than I'm going to pay you for a difference in these two cars." He didn't argue with me. He didn't get defensive. He didn't try to justify the price.

With an almost casual confidence, old Chuck looked at me as he put the ball back in my court. That's, after all, where the decision is going to be. Sales point number ten is this: Don't argue. Don't get defensive or try to justify the price at that point. Give the ball back to the prospect.

So, pleasantly and gently, old Chuck stayed on the offense. "Mr. Ziglar, what do you think would be a fair exchange between your nice, clean four-year-old Regency Oldsmobile and our gorgeous new Cadillac Sedan DeVille?"

Sales point number eleven: use the Abraham Lincoln approach. That's what Chuck was doing. You might recall that when Abraham Lincoln was a courtroom attorney, a lot of times he would represent both sides of the story. In other words, he would try both sides of the case, and he would always say good things about the opposition. As a matter of fact, sometimes the other attorney said that Abe had a better case for their side than he had developed themselves, but Abe obviously saved the most eloquent for his own client.

Notice what old Chuck's doing. He's saying good things about my previous purchase, but he's saying eloquent things about his own product, and that's what you need to do. What did old Chuck say? He said "a nice, clean, four-year-old Oldsmobile Regency," and when he's talking about his car, "that gorgeous new Cadillac." When he'd say *Cadillac*, you could just feel the difference there. Sedan DeVille.

Sales point number twelve is this: defend the prospect's previous purchase, even if the prospect says ugly things about it. You rise above it. If the prospect says, "Man, when I got this, they just saw me coming. They really took advantage of me," and if you agree—"Yes, they kind of did get you"—you know what the prospect is going to think? They're going to think, "Yes, that last dude got to me, but I'll guarantee you, friend, you are not going to get to me."

What is the proper thing to say? Very simply this. Regardless of how ugly the prospect has talked about a previous purchase or experience, you simply say, "Well, you know, Mr. Prospect, at the time you made that decision, when circumstances were such as they were, you used the information you had, and I guarantee you that many, many of us would have done exactly the same thing that you did."

There will never be an individual who will not say to you, "Yes, there have been times I bought something and was excited about it, and then later realized I had really not made a wise return." When you buy anything significant, we've all felt like we were making the right decision.

Let's look back at the question. "What do you think, Mr. Ziglar, would be a fair exchange between these two cars?" This is sales point number thirteen. At this point Chuck Bellows had invested something like twenty-five minutes with me. As a professional, he needs to find out if I really am a legitimate prospect. Twenty-five minutes is fine, but you can't invest that much time with everybody if they are not going to turn out to be prospects. You need to find out if you're in the same ballpark or if you're in different ball games.

For example, if I seriously say to him, "Well, Chuck, I think $500 would be enough," he's obviously wasting his time. If a house has a listing price of $250,000 and your prospect offers $95,000, they're just kidding you and themselves. You do not have a serious prospect. Chuck needs to find that out.

At that point, I reached over and took the talking pad out of Chuck's hand, and I said, "Chuck, I've always believed in round figures, and I believe that $7000 would be a gosh-awful plenty to pay for that car in exchange, and that includes the tax and all the other charges."

Chuck said calmly, quietly, and seriously, "Mr. Ziglar, you asked the impossible. You're asking for a $385 discount. The taxes on it would be $350. That's $735. There's not a chance in a million that our company would go along with your offer." Then he said, "But in the unlikely event they should be prepared to accept your offer, are you prepared to drive this beautiful, new Cadillac Sedan DeVille home with you?"

All of the sudden it occurred to me that old boy is serious about selling, and it occurred to me that if somebody didn't do something, somebody's about to buy something from somebody. A lot of times when you've made an offer, or you've made an offer to accept an offer, a lot of people start to crawfish. That's exactly what I did.

I said, "I don't know about that, Chuck. I mean, $7000 is a lot of money, and I just don't have my money coming in that easy." Then, you see, my doubts entered the picture. Do I really want a Cadillac? Do I want green one? Do I want a four-door one? Do I want a Sedan DeVille? All of those thoughts entered my mind.

Here's what sales expert Charles Roth said as we make sales point number fourteen: at a major decision time, the prospect is temporarily insane. They are so excited or confused or puzzled, they don't know. At this point, the kind of person you are is infinitely more important than the kind of salesperson you are. Your integrity is so important because, you see, if the prospect doesn't trust you, he won't buy from you.

Let me emphasize a point here. Chuck had been working on me for over twenty years to sell me this car. Oh, I know what I said earlier, and you might think to yourself, "Wait a minute, Ziglar. A few minutes ago, you said you had just met him." Oh, I did, but Chuck Bellows had been working on me for over twenty years, because twenty years earlier, he had gone to work selling Cadillac automobiles for Roger Meier Cadillac.

Twenty years earlier, he had said, "I am going to make my career doing exactly this," and he knew that the only way he could build a career would be to deal right off the top of the deck. An incredibly high percentage of his sales is repeat business. You see, sales point number fifteen is this: the right kind of person in sales will train and study to develop professional sales skills.

That's what Chuck had been doing all of this time. So let's look at the sales skills Chuck developed. When he took the talking pad, for example, which I had taken back from him, and what he did was very simple. He scratched out that $7000, and he said, "Now, Mr. Ziglar, I don't think that there's a chance our company would go along with that offer." *Go along with* that offer? Again, he knows that that's good.

But he said, "Let's look at the $73-85. I know we'll go along with that offer because we've already made it." Then he smiled so gently and said, "Mr. Ziglar, we don't back out on our offers." Mildly dangerous, but only mildly, because our mutual friend had said to him, "Now, Chuck, you have to watch old Zig. He'd been known to pull both legs at the same time."

Sales point number sixteen is this. He was communicating a very important message to me. He was saying, "Mr. Ziglar, I'm not playing games with you. I'm serious about negotiating, and I expect you to be serious too."

At this point he went back to his talking pad. "Mr. Ziglar, we are offering you within $2600 of what you paid for your car," and he wrote the $2600. "Now that was well over four years ago. When you figure that, Mr. Ziglar," he said, "it's only cost you about $600 a year to drive that beautiful Oldsmobile." Then he lowered his voice, and with a twinkle in his eye, he said, "Mr. Ziglar, you can't drive a Chevrolet that cheap."

Sales point number seventeen: if the customer isn't buying, you might need to do more selling. Was he selling with that point? I'll tell you he was selling. I thought to myself, "Ziglar, you clever rascal. Other people pay $600 a year more to drive a low-price three, and here you are, driving this magnificent, great, big, old Regency Oldsmobile for just $600 a year."

Man, I really liked that. Then all of the sudden it hit me as to what he was doing. I took that pad away from him. I said, "Now, wait a minute, Chuck. Just wait a minute. I have offered you $7000 to swap cars, and that's it. That's all I'll give."

Chuck didn't giggle. He didn't smile. He didn't gloat or anything. He just simply stood there, and what he said—and this is sales point number eighteen: don't panic. Had Chuck tried to sell me on that $7000 figure when I started to crawfish, what I would have done is very simple. I would have, at that point, asked for a much lower price. Now I'm coming back, and I've said, "When I offered that $7000 to you, that's it."

As I said, Chuck didn't giggle or smile. You see, he understood a little sales psychology. He understood something about me. Dr. Hugh Russell in Atlanta,

Georgia, said this: "People don't always buy because they understand the offer. They will frequently buy because they feel like you understand them." Chuck didn't say, "Gotcha."

Sales point number nineteen is this: control your emotions. You need to be a poker player at a time like this, and at this point, old Chuck said to me very quietly, "Mr. Ziglar, this is out of my hands. I've gone as far as I can. I'll have to go back and talk to the appraiser." Notice now how he moves to my side of the table as he said, "But I just want you to know this: I really would love to have you as a customer. So let me assure you that I'll do everything I can to get your car at your price."

Notice: *your* car at *your* price. Sales point number twenty: get on the customer's side of the table. Sincerity, but that doesn't mean that you're abandoning the company. It simply means, as we will learn as we go along, that the sales process is not something you do *to* someone. It is something you do *with* or *for* someone.

Actually, if the customer and the company do not both win, ultimately it's going to be a losing situation for everyone. Sales point number twenty-one is that he was using a very subtle version of the assumptive close. He was talking about *my* car at *my* price. He was putting me in the driver's seat. He was putting me behind the wheel.

Sales point number twenty-two now takes place as Chuck begins to tie down the details. He said,

"Let me go talk to the appraiser, but before I talk to him, Mr. Ziglar, let me make absolutely certain that you and I are communicating and that I understand exactly what you are saying," and he turned to a new page.

"As I understand it, you will make the transaction provided the $7000 includes all taxes, all charges of all kind."

I said, "Chuck, you got it right. That's exactly it."

He went back to see the appraisers. He was only gone a couple of minutes. He came back and said, "You know, this is embarrassing to me, but the appraiser had an emergency arise. He's had to go home, and I just wonder, Mr. Ziglar, are you going to be able to sleep tonight not knowing whether or not you're going to own this magnificent new Cadillac today?"

I grinned and said, "I think maybe I'll be able to struggle through." But notice sales point number twenty-three as he ties down the sale. He said, "Now before you go, Mr. Ziglar, let me say this. In the automobile business, we don't even consider it a legitimate offer unless a deposit is made, but one thing I pride myself on after over twenty years in the automobile business is my ability to judge men of character. If I'm reading you right, when you say to me you'll agree if the $7000 includes all charges, you're a man of your word, your word is your bond, and that, tomorrow morning, if I can get that kind of an agreement, we're in business."

Now where's he putting me? "Are you a man of integrity, Mr. Ziglar?" Do you think for one moment I'm going to say, "No, Chuck, I'm a liar"? Uh-uh. So again I modestly admitted, "That's right, Chuck. If I give you my word on something, friend, you can absolutely count on it. My word is my bond."

I drove away. The next morning, when I walked in my office, the telephone was ringing. Chuck was on the other end, he was so excited, he was so enthused, and he said, "Mr. Ziglar, I have some wonderful news for you." He said, "I've talked to the appraiser. We really worked together, and we're going to be able to swap with you for just $7200."

I knew at that precise instant that I'd bought the car at my price because, as we'd say down home, you can put this in your little pipe and smoke it: when people compromise one time, whether it's on a price or a principle, the second compromise is just around the corner. I said, "Chuck, you know yesterday I was very much impressed with the fact that you gave me credit for being a man of my word. Yesterday I gave you my word I'd swap with you for $7000."

He said, "Mr. Ziglar, are you saying that is all you will give?"

"Chuck, we're not eyeballing, but we are communicating."

"I'll call you back in five minutes."

About forty-five seconds later, the telephone rang. "Mr. Ziglar, do you want me to bring this car to you, or would you come get it?"

I laughed and said, "Well, Chuck, I've always loved to have my cars brought to me."

"I'll see you in just a few minutes."

I'd like to cover sales point number twenty-four with you out of this example: if you're going to build a sales career, you have to keep in touch with your prospects.

Chuck called me regularly after that, especially the first few weeks, and the reason was very simple. Your new customers, those who've just gotten what you've sold, almost regardless of what it is, are at their most enthusiastic best. They're excited. That's the time to get the prospects from them.

The truth is, you will never survive in the sales world over a period of years until and unless you can get your customers helping you sell more merchandise. You'll burn out, you'll wear out. But if you get those enthusiastic customers to give you leads and encouragement, that's the way you build your career.

Sales point number twenty-five is this one: When I drove in for the first service call, the first person I saw was Chuck Bellows. He greeted me warmly. "Mr. Ziglar, it is a delight to see you. Thank goodness you're in for service. Let me go with you to the service department. I personally want to introduce you to the service manager, and I want to make absolutely certain that every need you have is taken care of."

Chuck understood that service to that customer is extremely important. You see, it is true. You can have everything in life you want if you just help enough other people get what they want.

I believe that this story contains many valid and useful points and lots of information that will make a difference, but now is when the training really starts. You take your support materials, and you and your staff, you drill and practice and rehearse, and use all of these things until they become a part of you. That's one of the most important secrets in successful selling.

CHAPTER

2

The Heart of Your Sales Career

Zig

Sometimes it's the little things that make a big difference. It is the part of the blanket that hangs over the bed that keeps you warm. I read something not too long ago that every merchant and every salesperson on the face of this earth should read on a regular basis:

> *I'm your customer who never comes back. I'm a nice customer. All merchants know me. I'm the one who never complains, no matter what kind of service I get. When I go to a store to buy something, I don't throw my weight around. I try to be thoughtful of the other person. If I get a snooty clerk who gets upset because I want to look at several things before I make up my mind, I'm as polite as can be. I don't believe rudeness in return is the answer. I never kick, complain, or criticize, and I wouldn't*

dream of making a scene, as I've seen people doing in public places.

No, I'm the nice customer, but I'm also the nice customer who never comes back. That's my little revenge for being abused and taking whatever you hand out, because I know I'm not coming back. This way it doesn't immediately relieve my feelings, but in the long run, it's far more satisfying than blowing my top. In fact, a nice customer like myself, multiplied by others of my kind, can ruin a business, and there are a lot of nice people just like me.

When we get pushed far enough, we go to another store, where they appreciate nice customers. He laughs best, they say, who laughs last. I laugh when I see you frantically advertising to get me back when you could have kept me in the first place with a few kind words and a smile.

Your business might be in a different town, and your situation might be different, but if your business is bad, chances are good that if you will change your attitude, the word will get around, and I'll change from the nice customer who never comes back to the nice customer who always comes back and brings his friends.

I want to share with you what we believe is the very heart of your sales career. The first point I wish to make is the importance of honesty.

The Forum Corporation out of Boston, Massachusetts did a study of 341 salespeople: 173 of them were outstandingly successful, 168 of them were moderately successful. They came from eleven different companies in five different industries. They'd sold everything from real estate and insurance to industrial supplies and what have you. All of them had sold at least five years, so we can eliminate the rookie factor.

They discovered that the one thing that separated these salespeople may be a little surprising to you. All of them had the same basic experience. Each knew how to get prospects, each knew how to get appointments, each knew how to make presentations demonstrating features and benefits, each knew how to handle objections and close sales, and yet one group was dramatically more successful than the other.

The basic reason has to do with one word: *honesty*. You see, this group had trust. Their customers trusted them. What they discovered is this: People don't buy based on what you tell them. They do not buy based on what you show them. They *do* buy based on what you tell them and what you show them that they believe.

Whom are they going to believe? They're going to believe the good guys, and they're going to believe the good gals.

The second thing they discovered about the outstanding salespeople was this: They realize that, since they did not have secretaries and administrative assistants, they had to work through everybody in the home office. So they understood that the sale is not complete, it really isn't sold, until the product has been delivered, installed, serviced, and paid for, and the customer is satisfied.

So when they called in, the supersalespeople were just as nice to the switchboard operator as they were to the chairman of the board. They were just as kind and thoughtful and gracious to the file clerks and the shipping clerks as they were to the corporate executives. They all were working together.

Yes, the heart of your sales career starts with the word *honesty*.

The late Charles Roth said this: "People feel that if they utter the three magic words *business is business*, they have license to lie, cheat, steal, and in general, rape their fellow man. The fear that those things will happen often exist in the mind of the prospect."

Roth pointed out that a calm, confident, positive, reassuring salesperson, working from a base of honesty and integrity, is the most effective tool for calming the fears of the prospect and get the sale.

Yes, honestly is a prerequisite for a successful career in selling.

When I am on tour, a lot of times the media will ask me, "Mr. Ziglar, is it really true that you could sell anybody anything?" That's insane. Only a con artist can sell anybody anything. The real professional can only sell those things he or she truly believes are going to benefit the prospect more than the money they will receive will benefit the professional.

The second part of the heart of your sales career has to do with ego. Dr. H.M. Greenberg, a New Jersey psychologist, did an evaluation on 186,000 people over a period of years. He discovered that one person in five walking down the street at any given time of day could be trained to be successful in the world of selling. But he also discovered that the people who were the most successful had a most unusual kind of ego.

It's the kind of ego that demands acceptance. When that person gets the appointment, that soothes and strokes their ego. When they make the presentation, if the reception is good, that feeds their ego. When they close the sale, that's the prospect's way of saying, "I like you, and I trust you."

But Greenberg also discovered that if this salesperson *only* had ego, watch out, because a lot of times they'll stretch the truth to make the sale. He said, "Give me that individual with a good, healthy ego, but who has empathy to go along with it."

There's a lot of difference between sympathy and empathy. *Sympathy* simply means that you feel the way the other person feels. *Empathy* means that you understand how they feel, but you don't feel that way. Because you don't feel that way but do understand how they feel, you can back away from the problem and offer the solution. I want to emphasize this: sympathy costs sales, but empathy creates sales.

Let me give you an example. Many years ago, in 1962, I was the number-one cookware salesman in our country. I was with the Saladmaster Corporation from Dallas. I was living in Columbia, South Carolina. I was selling to everybody in sight.

One day I was over visiting with an associate, who also represented the company. We did not represent the same part of the organization. He was starving to death, and as we sat there and talked and he was singing the blues, I said, "Well, Bill, I know what your problem is."

"Tell me quick," he said. "I have to make sales."

"The problem is simple. You do not believe in what you're selling."

Bill about blew a gasket. He said, "What are you talking about? I left a company I'd been with over five years as a manager to come with this company as a salesperson because the product is so much better."

"Bill," I said, "peddle that baloney to somebody else. I know and I know that you know you don't believe in this product." With that, I nodded toward the stove.

"You mean the fact that I'm cooking in a competitive set of cookware?"

"Exactly."

"Oh, Zig," he said, "don't let that enter your mind. Nothing could be further from the truth. I believe we have the greatest set of cookware on the American market, but, Zig, I've had some difficulties. My wife's been in the hospital, and when she's in there, she's there two weeks. You can't half work. You worry.

"I wrecked my car, and for six weeks I had to borrow transportation. You can't sell when you have to depend on a taxi and borrowed cars and all. Now it looks like we're going to have to put the boys in the hospital and get their tonsils out. I don't even have any insurance, but," he said, "Zig, I'm going to get a set of the cookware."

"Bill," I said, "let me ask you. How long have you been with this company?"

"Five years."

"What was your problem last year and the year before that and the year before that?" I said, "Bill, let me tell you exactly what happens. When you're in a closing situation, and you get down in the short rows, and you ask the obligating question, I can see it now.

"The prospect looks to you and says, 'Oh I don't know, Bill. Doggonit, I always sure need to buy a good set of pots, but now is not the right time. You know, Bill, my wife's been in the hospital a couple of weeks, and man, you can't half work when your wife's in the hospital and you're worrying about it. We wrecked the car not too long ago, and for six weeks we had to depend on borrowed transportation, and you just can't have to do things that way. And now it looks like we're going to have to put the boys in the hospital, and we don't even have any insurance.'

"Bill, you and I both know no prospect is ever going to give you the same things you gave me, but they *are* going to bring up excuses you've been using for years, and you're a positive thinker. I know you're sitting there saying to yourself, 'Now, think positive, Bill, think positive, Bill, think positive.' But all the time, deep in your mind, you're thinking to yourself, 'I know what you're talking about. I don't have a set of the stuff myself.'

"Bill, if you don't ever hear me say another thing, hear me when I say this: Selling is nothing in this world but a transference of feeling. If I can make you feel about the product I'm selling like *I* feel about the product I'm selling, you will buy my product. You *must* own a set of this cookware. If you have to mortgage your furniture, do it."

He said, "Do you really think it's that important?"

I said, "I *know* it is that important."

To bring this story to a close, I sold him a set of the cookware. Obviously he wrote his own order, but that week, Bill made enough extra sales to completely pay for that set of cookware.

Why was that? Very simple. He knew that he had sacrificed. He knew that he had had to dig deep in order to make the purchase, and then when the prospect would start giving the objections, Bill could honestly, sincerely, and conscientiously say, "Yes, indeed, it's fully worth whatever the price is. It'll make a difference in your home." You see, for a long time, sympathy had been costing Bill sales.

On the other side of the ledger, what's empathy? A good friend of mine, Jay Martin, is the president of a company out of Memphis, Tennessee. They sell smoke and fire detectors and water purification.

Jay was telling me about working one evening with a young dealer, who made the sales presentation. When he finished and asked the obligating question, the old boy rocked back on the two hind legs of the chair, folded his arms, and in his own colloquialism manner said, "Well, son, I'm sure you heard about my wreck." The young salesman hadn't heard about the wreck, but he was about to.

The customer said, "Me and my wife were going down the road one night, and this fellow passed on the wrong side, hit us both head-on and tore our car all to pieces. Put us both in the hospital. I was in there about ten days. It left my leg a little bit stiff. I work on piece goods, so my income's down a little bit, and that sure doesn't help anything.

"My wife was in the hospital six weeks. She was gone so long, as a matter of fact, they phased her job out. Now there ain't but one of us working, and when you've been accustomed to having two incomes, that sure knocks you for a loop.

"The insurance bill for everything we were doing was over $20,000. Now I know the insurance company's going to pay for it, but they sure have us nervous in the meantime. Then last week, our boy came home from the Navy, and the first night back, he rounded a curve too fast, ran over a steep embankment, ran down into a service station, wrecked the car, tore up a $7000 sign. Now I know our insurance is going to pay for the car, but I don't know if it's going to pay for that sign. If it doesn't, man, we're going to be in trouble.

"Just last night, we had to put my wife's mother in the most expensive nursing home in the county, and the only method of support outside of me is her brother, and he ain't been heard from in seven or eight years. It ain't worth shooting if we did know where he was. I don't know how we're going to handle that deal."

Now, that's a whole lot of trouble. If the young salesman had sympathy, he'd be saying, "Oh, that's too bad. I know that is a tough thing, but won't the government help you? How about the Red Cross? Won't some of your neighbors chip in? Won't the church do something? Can't you get food stamps? Isn't there something you can do?" That's sympathy.

The young man had empathy. It meant he understood how he felt, but it meant also that he was able to back away from the problem and look at the solution. As a salesman, he acted like a pro. He looked right at the prospect, and he said, "Tell me, Mr. Prospect, in addition to those things, would there be any other reason why you could not go ahead and install this equipment in your home?"

The old boy just about had a conniption. He just hollered. He slapped his leg, and he said, "No, son. Those are all the problems."

The young salesman simply reached out in his sample case. He picked up one of the smoke detectors, and they have what they call the *physical action close*. He moved over to show the prospect exactly how it would look on the wall, and he said to him, "Sir, from what you tell me, you now owe nearly $30,000, and $300 more won't make any difference at all."

The thing that got the sale was this. He said, "Sir, fire under any circumstances is devastating, but in your case, it would wipe you out." Don't miss that other significant sales lesson, which was this: He had taken the reasons, all of them, that the man had given him for why they could *not* buy and used them as reasons why they *must* buy. Almost without exception, you can take the reason they give you for not buying and use it as the reason why they should go ahead and buy.

The third part of the heart of your sales career has to do with your *attitude*. I will say it over and over. Business is never either good or bad out there. Business is either good or bad right here between your own two ears.

Down in the little town of Victoria, Texas, there's an insurance salesman named Calvin Hunt. Calvin is the man who goes the extra mile, understanding that you can have everything you want in life if you will just help enough other people get what they want.

Once a year he will bring in speakers from all over America, pay them their full fees, and invite all of his clients to come in for an evening of inspiration. He lets them sit at the front of the big auditorium. Everybody else can come as they please and sit where they please, but the front-row seats are held for his clients.

He uses it as a community project. It's a marvelous way to create a tremendous amount of goodwill.

Calvin and I were talking about 1982, which was a recession year, and I said, "Calvin, how is your business?"

"You know, Zig," he said, we have a recession going on in the minds of some people, but I decided not to join. Actually, we do 98 or 95 percent as much insurance business today as we did last year. But the average insurance salesman figures that during the recession, people are not going to be in a buying mood, so about half of them don't really work."

So, he said, "Here's the way I figured it, Zig. I figured that if half the competition was gone, and we had 95 percent as much business still available, that surely I could at least double my business during the year." Interestingly, that's exactly what he did.

Calvin is an unusual insurance man. He sells those contracts where the premium is in excess of $100,000 a year. I haven't talked to Calvin since 1986, so I don't know what he's doing at this precise moment, but I can tell you this, 1986 was the biggest year he's ever had in the insurance business, unless this year he happens to be doing better. Positive thinking, your attitude—it is so important.

What is positive thinking, and what is positive believing? Positive thinking, according to my definition, is an optimistic hope, not necessarily based on any facts, that you can move some mountains. I've seen positive thinkers move some mountains. I've also seen them get their teeth kicked in on occasion, including in the sales world, but I'd rather have a positive thinker than a negative thinker.

What is a positive believer? A positive believer is an individual who has that same optimistic hope, but this time with reasons for believing they can move those mountains.

In the world of sales, contrary to what people think, things are not anywhere close to being equal. The opportunities are, but the salesperson who goes out there to sell who doesn't know how to prospect, who doesn't know how to get appointments, who does not know how to make a good presentation, who does not know how to close, who does not know how to handle objections—in other words, the one who has not acquired professional skills—by no stretch of imagination does that salesperson have the same opportunity for success as the others.

Training is a significant key. Positive believing means you've utilized and taken advantage of the training, the books, the tapes, the seminars, the sessions, the programs your company has to offer that will make a difference. Yes, positive believers will sell more than just positive thinkers.

The next part of the heart of your sales career has to do with your *reserve*. There are three kinds of reserve. There's physical reserve. It requires a lot of energy to sell.

I happen to believe that your physical condition is extraordinarily important. The average salesperson works about eight hours a day. The first seven hours of the day, they spend working for everybody else. They make the house payments with what they earn, their car payments, they take care of the insurance and food and clothing and all the other things.

The last hour, that salesperson ought to be working for themselves. The problem is, by the end of the day, too many of them, as we'd say down home, are too pooped to pop. They have run out of energy. You need to build physical reserve.

There are some basics there. You need to take care by eating the proper diet. You need to get a reasonable amount of sleep. You need to get involved in an exercise program. You need to stop putting poison in your body. You know what booze and smoking and drugs do to the body? This is not the time or the place for me to talk about those things, but I want to emphasize that when you do take care of your physical body, you will be dramatically surprised at the difference in your sales results.

Fifteen years ago, I got on a diet and exercise program. It dramatically increased my energy level, and I can work considerably longer today than I could when I was twenty-five years old. Build a physical reserve. Build a mental reserve.

One thing I can never understand is a salesperson who does not have their own cassette programs and their own cassette recorders. When you're in your car, on your way to calls or on the way to your office or on your way to work, you should be listening. On your way home, or if you work from your car between calls, you need to be listening, and the most important time to listen is the first thing in the morning.

You obviously need to be reading and studying, but psychologists say that the first person you encounter each day has more impact on your attitude than the next five people you encounter. Choose somebody who inspires you. Start the day with an inspirational recording and listen on your way to that first call. It will make a difference. Build that mental reserve.

You also need to build a spiritual reserve. I learned something not too long ago, which, to me, was astonishing, and yet it really wasn't. It was delightful to learn. I learned, for example, that everybody believes in God. Now, that might surprise you just a little bit when I say that, but yes, everybody does believe in God.

I was talking with the chairman of the board of a major trucking line, which has in excess of 300 terminals and offices throughout America. They conduct a lie detector test on each new employee.

One of the questions that they asked, and they've asked it thousands of times is this. "Do you believe there is a God?" In every single case, when the prospect said no, that needle on the polygraph just jumped off the chart. Every time they said no, the polygraph said they lied about it.

Build a spiritual reserve. It can make a difference.

The final thing we're going to talk about is, you have to be tough. This is probably going to surprise you, but the toughest thing in the world of selling, the toughest thing, the thing I believe is the most important here, is love.

It might surprise you to hear me talking about love as part of a sales career, but I'm willing to talk about it by telling you a story. I love to play golf. Anybody who knows me knows I love to get out there and hit that little golf ball. There's nothing I enjoy anymore than teeing that dude up and raring back and really getting after it. Boom.

I found out a long time ago that a fast game of golf and a slow game of golf both require about five hours, and when you're gone as much as I'm gone, I'm not about to go home and kiss that redhead and my son good-bye. (I have three daughters also, but he came ten years after our last daughter was born.) I'm not about to go home and kiss that redhead and that boy good-bye and head for the golf course, but I love to play golf.

One day I came up with a brilliant idea. I bought my wife and my son a set of golf clubs. Everybody was excited about it except my wife and my son. They went along with me for about five games. End of the fifth game, the redhead said, "Honey, I just don't like to play golf."

Incidentally, when I talk about my wife, I call her the redhead. When I'm talking to her, it's "sugar baby." Her name is Jean.

One day after about the fifth game, she said, "Honey, I just don't like to play golf. It's too hot, or it's too cold, or it's too wet, or it's too dry, or too something. It's just not my game. Count me out."

There went golf buddy number one. End of the summer, my boy said to me, "Dad, I don't know how to tell you this, because I know how much you like to play golf, and I know you like to be with me, Dad, and I like to be with you, too, but Dad, golf's just not my game. I'll play football with you, I'll go to the games with you. I'll play catch with you. I'll go fishing with you, but golf is just not my game, Dad."

For the next three years, there wasn't much golf in my life. Then one night, I was back in town in the middle of the week right here in Dallas, Texas, over on North Central Expressway, when the old driving range was still there. We'd been out to dinner. My sticks were in the trunk of the car. We rode past the driving range, and all of a sudden, my boy said, "Dad, let's stop and hit a few."

My boy was a smooth talker, so we stopped to hit a few. We were banging away, and after a couple of minutes, he said, "Dad, let me borrow one of your woods." So, I handed my son the four wood. He choked up on it a little bit. He reared back. He let a string out. He busted that dude right down the middle about forty yards further than he'd ever hit a golf ball before in his life.

When he turned around, I knew I had myself my golfing buddy. The second most beautiful smile I'd ever seen on that face. The most beautiful one was two days later.

We were out at the club playing. He took that four wood. Again, he choked up. He let the string out. He pole-axed that dude right down the middle. It had a little draw on it. Hit the ground running like a scared rabbit, stopped dead center right in the middle of the fairway. Perfect position.

We got to it. He took his five iron out, and just like you see them doing on television, he kept his head down. He smooth-stroked that ball. It took off and got right over the green. It landed just as soft as a feather about forty feet from the pin. He's hunting his bird.

That means if he sinks the putt, he's one under par on this hole. If that doesn't mean anything to you, it simply means he done good.

I showed the boy how to align the putt. I showed him how to stroke the ball, and when he stroked that putt, the instant he stroked it, there never was any doubt about it. It was in the cup all the way. When that ball hit the bottom of that cup, that boy jumped straight up about six feet, still beating me to the ground by five seconds.

You're talking about excitement. I was excited. He was excited. I grabbed him, and we hugged there for about two minutes, and all of a sudden it dawned on me I had a problem. You see, I was on the green in two also. I was hunting my bird. I was only about ten feet from the cup. I knew if I missed it, my son would figure I had done it on purpose, which would have given him a cheap victory.

So I determined I was going to do the very best I could, so that if I did miss, I could honestly say to my son, "Congratulations, son. You've won it fair and square."

I aligned the putt as carefully as I'd ever aligned a putt in my life. I stroked the putt, and just like it had eyes, it went straight to the bottom of the cup. Before I reached down to pick it up, I looked at my son, and I said, "Now, son, tell me the truth. Were you pulling for Dad?"

I think you know what it would have meant had I missed. He was eleven years old. He had never beaten his dad in a hole of golf. It would have meant a tremendous amount, yet quietly, without any hesitation, and very firmly, my son looked me right in the eye and said, "Dad, I always pull for you."

Now that's what we need more of in Dallas, Texas, and Portland, Oregon, and Buffalo, New York, and Washington, D.C. It's what we need in every home in every county in every state in this great land of ours. It's what we need between the parent and the child, the husband and the wife, the teacher and the student. Surprisingly enough, it's what we need between the salesperson and the prospect.

Yes, it is, because when you are selling to someone, and they are weighing their decision, your belief in what you're selling and the benefits it will give to them should be so strong that you're pulling for them to buy for their own benefit.

If you can honestly and sincerely do that, then your career will catapult upwards, because it is absolutely true, as a wise man said so long ago, that people don't care how much you know until they know how much you care, and you can persuade through your heart. The right procedures, the right techniques, the right words, the right voice inflection can make a difference.

As we conclude, you'll notice that we talked about honesty, ego, attitude, reserve, and toughness, and if you will simply take the first letter of each of these words, you will see that it forms an acronym for *heart,* because the truth is, if your heart is all right, then your career is going to be all right. That's one of the real secrets of successful selling.

Success Sales Psychology

Zig

I was conducting sales training and motivational classes for a company from 9:00 in the morning until 9:00 in the evening, six days a week.

That's about as busy as you can get. I did not have time to go look for a house, and with three children in a motel room with your wife, that really is kind of crowded, so the redhead and I talked about a house. At great length, we talked about the house.

We finally decided on what was a reasonable price. Now I know the price was reasonable because she explained to me that it was reasonable. It looked like the foreign-aid bill for the world to me, but she assured me everything was all right.

She went out and searched for a house, and to give her full credit, she really looked at two houses. When she walked in the front door of that second one, the search had ended. She had found what she was looking for.

You need to understand our discussion about that house. We had agreed on a certain price, and then all of a sudden, she said to me, "Honey, suppose we find the dream home—I mean exactly what we're looking for—will that end our house hunting for all time? How much more can we invest than that original amount we talked about?'

We wrestled with that one over and over, and we finally arrived at a figure which was an additional $20,000. I know what you're thinking. "In today's market? $20,000? What are you, Ziglar, the last of the big spenders?"

Let me explain that in Dallas in 1968 you could buy quality housing, after you had your lot, for around $10 or $11 a square foot. So when I'm talking about an additional $20,000, I'm talking about a bunch of house extra.

Today for another $20,000 you could get a neat little carport or a small patio, but in those days it was a whole lot, so that's what she went out looking for, and when she came back after looking at that second house, she had found what she was looking for. I remember it as if it were yesterday.

I walked in the motel room that evening a little after 9:00, when I'd finished the session, and she was seated on that king-size bed, and she was so excited the bed was vibrating. She hopped up, and she ran over to me, and she said, "Honey, I have found the house. It absolutely is magnificent, in a real nice section of town, has four nice bedrooms on a great big lot, huge garage."

"Well, sweetheart," I said, "how much does this house cost?"

"Aww, honey, you're going to have to see it," she said. "Every single bedroom has a walk-in closet. It has four baths, and the backyard is plenty big enough for you to build that arrow-shaped swimming pool that you've been talking about. The master bedroom is so big we're going to have to get us a riding vacuum cleaner. Honey, it is absolutely magnificent."

I said, "Sweetheart, how much does that house cost?"

I finally got it out of her. She told me, and it was $18,000 more than the maximum, which we had already agreed, at least in my mind, was $20,000 more than we had any business at all to spend or to invest.

"Sweetheart," I said, "we cannot invest that much money in a house."

"I know that, sweetheart," she said, "but you know, we really don't know anything about real-estate values here in Dallas, so I did ask the builder to stop by tomorrow evening when you finish your class and take us all out to see that house at the same time, so you can get a feel for the market."

"I'll go and look at it, but I just want you to know in advance, that's all we're going to do so we can get a benchmark to go from."

"Don't worry about it," she said.

Sales lesson number one is simply this: when possible, you establish value before you give price. That's very important. If you'll notice, she told me about the bedroom, she told me about the walk-in closets, she told all about that huge master bedroom, she told me where I could build a swimming pool, she told me about the neighborhood. Try to establish value before you give the price.

Sales lesson number two comes right behind it: you always establish value before you ask for the order. If you don't, you come across as a high-pressure salesperson who wants to make the sale quickly or get rid of the prospect so you can get out of there and see somebody else. No, you establish value before you ever ask for the order.

Sales lesson number three is this: you get the prospect involved with the product as quickly as possible. She had said, "The builder's coming by. We're going to go out, and we're going to look at that house."

The next evening, when we pulled up in the driveway, I knew I had a problem. It was exactly what I was looking for—a beautiful neighborhood, a wonderful-looking, ranch-type home.

At that point, I did something that your prospects have been doing to you all of your life, and that brings us up to sales lesson number four. Please remember this: your best prospects are the toughest ones to get the appointment with.

Why did I resist going out there to see this gorgeous house? I knew from what she had said that it sounded like exactly what I wanted, and I did not want to go see that house at that point, because I was afraid of something, which brings us to lesson number five in the world of selling, and that is, when we walked in that house, I acted as if I had no interest at all.

You see, your best prospects often show no interest. Why in the world would I indicate to that redhead I had no interest in that house?

The reason is very simple. I was afraid that if I showed any enthusiasm at all, the redhead and that builder would gang up on me and talk me into doing something I already wanted to do, knew I had no business doing, and was scared I was going to do if I gave them any encouragement at all—buy a house that I did not feel we could afford to invest in.

As we walked through the front door, an interesting thing happened. There was a nice little entranceway with a neat little chandelier. Now the redhead has never had dramatic training. But as we walked in, she just looked over her shoulder ever so slightly, paused approximately one-half second, glanced up at that beautiful chandelier, and walked on. Message delivered. Message received.

When she walked into the den, she immediately started giving me ownership of the whole thing. She said, "Honey, look at what a big, beautiful den this is, and look, honey, this gorgeous fireplace, and you notice all the bookshelves, which you can put all of your books in? Over here, honey, we're going to set the television set, and I can see you now with our big, oversized sofa here, which there's plenty of room in this den for. I can see you laying on that sofa on Sunday afternoon watching the Cowboys out of one eye and watching that fire burn in your fireplace out of the other eye."

Then she said, "Look back here," and she took me all over that house. We got into the master bedroom, and she said, "See what I told you, honey? Plenty of room. We can put the king-size bed over here, and you know how you and I like to get up in the morning and drink coffee. We'll sit at a little table over here with our chairs here. There's plenty of room. Now, honey, just look at your closet. I mean, even as messy as you are, there's plenty of room for everything right in here for all of your clothes in your closet."

She opened the back door and walked out and said, "You see what the backyard looks at. I measured it all. We can put one end of the pool up here, and we can put another end of the pool right down here, and then we'll go right into the big garage. Look, honey, plenty of room there for your two cars, and if you'll notice, here is a place, 11 x 11, where we can build that little office you've been talking about."

Yes, she was really giving my ownership all the way through, and that is sales lesson number six. Finally, when the tour of the house was over, we stood there, she reached over, and she squeezed my hand,

and she looked up into my eyes, all five feet of her, and said, "Honey, how do you feel about this home?"

That's sales lesson number seven. You ask the prospect how they feel, not what they think. Interestingly enough, people buy emotionally. They buy with their heart, not with their head. How do you feel? I said, "Well, sweetheart, it's beautiful."

What else could I say? I mean, there I was. You think I'm going to look down at that smiling face looking up into my eyes and say, "No, I don't like this house. It's just a wild idea you got." No way, so I said, "Sweetheart, it's absolutely gorgeous. I would love to have it, but you know we cannot invest in a home this expensive."

"I knew that, honey," she said, "but I just wanted you to see something which was really nice. Now we'll go look at something cheap." Come on, you don't think she's trying to shame me into doing anything, do you? She's not that kind of a girl.

Nothing else was said that night, and actually that is sales lesson number eight. Sometimes you need to back away. Sometimes you need to let that prospect breathe when you have the luxury of doing so.

Now when would that be? On this occasion, obviously we're going to be together the next morning. If you have a ride back to the office or something of that nature and your prospect is still with you, let them breathe and collect their breath. Sometimes they're letting the facts soak in and they're mulling in their minds as to whether or not or how could they handle this particular situation.

The next morning I was in the bathroom, brushing my teeth, and when you have a mouthful of toothbrush, you're handicapped, at least as far as your speech is concerned. She walked in and said, "Honey, how long do you think we're going to live in Dallas?"

I said, "A hundred years."

"How long?"

"A hundred years. I love Dallas. I hate to move. This is centrally located. This is where I want to stay."

"No, I mean really how long do you think we're going to live here?"

"From here on in. I love this city."

"You really think, then, we'll be here thirty years?"

"Absolutely. Why do you ask?"

"Honey," she said, "you know I was just thinking about that $18,000." She forgot all about the $20,000. I say she forgot. I wonder, did she? She forgot about the original price of the home, interest and taxes and insurance. She said, "That $18,000 spread over thirty years; now how much would that be a year?"

"That would be $600 a year."

"How much would that be a month?"

"Well, $600 a year, that's about $50 a month."

Then she said, "How much will that be a day?"

"Sweetheart, come on," I said. "Your arithmetic is just as good as mine. That would come out to about $1.70 a day. Why do you ask me all of these questions?"

"I was just wondering if you would be willing to invest another $1.70 a day to have a happy wife instead of just a wife."

Guess where we lived for seventeen years? That's right.

I want to establish something very important. She did not let the *why* we should buy serve as a stumbling block to the *how* we could buy it. Now, you might wonder, "Now, Zig, is your wife a salesperson? Is she in selling?"

She doesn't have a briefcase, and she doesn't go out and sell, nor does she work in a store where people come in to see her, but I'm here to tell you that everybody on the face of this earth is in the world of selling, and everybody is, in fact, a salesperson.

You might wonder, "Where did she learn that particular thing?"

In the afternoon, during these training classes I was teaching right there in the motel, when our daughters would get home, they'd look after our son while he was taking a nap. She would come into the training rooms, and she heard me talking about this. That close, incidentally, is what we call the *1902*. In 1902 a man named Frederick Sheldon wrote a book, and in the book he talked about that.

Sales lesson number nine out of this story is this: even though I am knowledgeable about sales training and technique, really good technique in the hands of a really good person is extremely effective.

Sales lesson number ten is that she made it afford-able. How could I honestly say I could not come up with another $1.70 a day? Obviously I knew it would be more than $1.70 a day. But the professional sales-person always makes it easy for the prospect to buy. That is exactly what she was doing.

Sales lesson number eleven, incidentally, is to know how to ask a lot of questions.

Sales lesson number twelve: you need to under-stand what your sales objective is when you make a sales call. You might say, "Ziglar, that's crazy. Every-body knows that. The objective of a sales call is to make a sale." Everybody does understand that, but what kind of a sale? What price sale? She clearly understood what her objective was. It was to make an $18,000 sale. Oh, the house cost a whole lot more than that, but that was her objective—to make an $18,000 sale. Before we ever left the house, she had already sold the original price. She had already sold the additional $20,000 that the house was going to cost. Now all she needed to do was make that $18,000 sale.

That's extraordinarily important. Let's say you're in the automobile business and a couple comes in, and they say to you, "Look, our payments cannot exceed more than $400 a month if we're going to be able to trade with you." You find exactly what they need and exactly what they want, but the payments come to $475 a month. Now you have a $75 a month sale in front of you. You see, they had bought the $400 before you even entered the picture. You had nothing to do with that. Their needs and wants had already established the $400, just like in real estate.

If, for example, a couple says to you, "Look, $250,000, that's it. That's max. That's as far as we can go. Here's what we want for it." They detail exactly what they want for that $250,000. You find exactly what they want, but the price is $280,000. You don't have to make a $280,000 sale. You have to make a $30,000 sale.

Why is that so important? Because psychologically, and from your perspective, it's easier to sell that other $30,000 than it is the total $280,000.

Sales lesson number thirteen is this: you need to know as much as possible about your prospect. Obviously, since we had been married for many, many years, she had a chance to know an awful lot about me. You are never going to be able to get that well-acquainted with all of your prospects. You can't work on somebody for thirty or forty years to make a sale and expect to survive in the world of selling unless you're selling some powerful expensive products out there.

What am I getting at? She knew one thing that I very much wanted in life. When I was a youngster in Yazoo City, Mississippi, I was invited one day by a buddy of mine to go swimming at the country club. It was a hot day that summer. I rode my bicycle out to the club. I had on my bathing suit. Man, I was ready to hop in, but my buddy never showed. There wasn't another person around. The water looked so cool and inviting, I could not resist it, and in that pool I went.

I knew I had no business doing that. You can't go in unless you're with a member. I'd been in that pool no more than two minutes when this fellow who was a member and who traded at the store where I worked, came by, playing golf, and saw me in there. He knew I had no business in that club. He told me to come see him the next day.

I was scared to go see him. I was more afraid *not* to go see him. To this day, I vividly remember that visit in his office. It was one of the toughest things I've ever done. That fellow, I thought, was awfully hard on me. I was afraid I was going to be put in jail.

When I left, there was tears in my eyes and my own childish anger and frustration. I said, "One of these days, I'm going to build me a swimming pool bigger than that one at the country club in Yazoo City, Mississippi." I'm here to tell you that in the summer of 1969, we built a swimming pool that was one foot longer than the original pool at that old country club.

Know as much about your prospect. She was capitalizing on that when she showed me where everything was.

Sales lesson number fourteen is this: don't miss the sale because you don't have what the prospect asked for. Did you know that a lot of times, the prospect asks for things that are not available? Put this one down and think on it.

A lot of people don't really know what they want because they don't know what is available. When we moved to Dallas from Columbia, South Carolina, I said, "Sweetheart, you're going to be spending most of the time at home, so you're going to select the home, but there are three things I do want. I do want a home with a swimming pool in it. I do want a little place where my office is going to be. I want that office in the home. I must be about writing some books. The third thing is I want a circle drive."

This home had an awful lot of things, but there were three things it did not have. It did not have the swimming pool. It did not have the office. It did not have the circle drive, and she used that as a sales plus. She said, "Look, honey. You can design your own pool. Here's where you can put your office. You can design your own circle drive."

Now I wanted that house, and we bought it. for a lot of different reasons.

There are five basic reasons why prospects *won't* buy from you. The first reason they won't buy from you is that in their minds they do not need what you're selling. I want to emphasize that salespeople are not needed to sell needs. You don't need salespeople.

Also how many television sets do you need? How many suits of clothes do you need? How many groceries do you need? We do not need anybody to sell needs.

When it gets beyond needs, there's something else. The second reason people don't buy is they don't have any money. It is true that some people do not have the money, and I don't want to mislead you or discourage you, but there are some people who lie to you about that one.

Let me tell you a fact: most people in corporations buy what they really want—not necessarily what they need, but what they want.

The third reason people don't buy is, they're in no hurry. As a young salesman, I read this poem and committed it to memory:

The bride, white of hair, is stooped over her cane.
Her footsteps, uncertain, need guiding,
While down the opposite church aisle,
With a wan, toothless smile
The bridegroom in a wheelchair comes riding.
Now who is this elderly couple thus wed?
You'll find when you've closely explored it
that here is that rare, most conservative pair
who waited till they could afford it.

The role of the professional salesperson is to impart a sense of urgency in the mind of the prospect, because there's seldom a perfect time to buy anything. You can't wait until all the lights are on green before you head for town. If you can impart to the prospect the idea that the major thing is to get started, and if they can handle this phase of it to begin with, yes, they can go ahead and enjoy ownership.

The fourth reason people don't buy is because they don't know what you're selling. That is so tough for us salespeople to understand. How could anybody not want this, as good as this is? They don't want it, though. That's where our opportunity comes in as salespeople.

Number five, they don't buy because they don't trust you. Very few of them are going to come out and say, "Look, friend, I know you're lying to me. You're exaggerating. It probably won't do all of those good things. That's impossible." Very few people are going to say that, but you will miss more sales because somewhere or other along the way, you have communicated something to that prospect that made them feel not quite right about buying. And you'll never know why.

That's why the most important part of the process is the salesperson. You can't be one kind of person and another kind of salesperson.

The prospect might buy you and still not buy the product, but he won't buy the product unless he has first bought you.

The sales process involves getting prospects. When you get a prospect, you're on first base. When you get the appointment, whether it's in person or on the telephone, you're on second base. When you make your presentation, you're on third base. So far nobody has sold anybody anything. All you've done is invest time and energy and effort and spent money.

Until you close the sale, you're nothing but a conversationalist.

Before we go any further, let me check your thinking on something. Do you feel you deserve a profit when you sell a product that solves a problem? OK. Do you feel you deserve two profits when you sell two products that solve two problems?

I'm not trying to put words in your mouth, because as the late Fred Herman would say, "That ain't sanitary," but you are saying that the more people you help, the more profit you deserve. You see, it is true: you can have everything in life you want if you will just help enough other people get what they want.

Next question. Say you've been selling for five years, or even a year. Do you still have customers who are using and enjoying the benefits of what you sold them a year ago or five years ago?

Who made the best deal, then? Was it the customer, or was it you? The customer made the best deal. That's right. You probably spent your profit in many cases even before you made the sale, but the question is, is the sales process something you do *to* somebody or *for* somebody?

I fought in the ring for a couple of years. As a matter of fact, the only reason I quit was because of my hands. The referee kept stepping on them. In the world of athletics, we go out, we try to find out where the opponent is weak, and we try to take advantage of the weakness. That's true whether it's in tennis, football, boxing, or what have you.

In the world of selling, we find out where the opponent, that is, the prospect, is weak—where he has a need. Then we strengthen their weakness by selling them what we are selling.

That's right. That's what professional selling is all about. But one of the most frustrating things you can do as a salesperson is convince a prospect and not persuade the prospect. You convince them that the merchandise is wonderful, and they agree. You convince them that it will save money. You convince them that they need it. You convince them that it will benefit them enormously, and that they have the money to buy it.

You've convinced them in every area, but they don't buy. "No, I don't think I'll take it." You've convinced but have not persuaded. Now where is the line?

Many years ago, a fellow named Aristotle, who was a very bright guy on most things, made a foolish statement. He said that if you drop two objects of different weights from the top of a tall building, they would fall at different rates of speed.

They'd been teaching that theory at the University of Pisa for a long time. Galileo came along and said, "That's crazy. Two objects will fall at exactly the same rate of speed, even if they're of different sizes."

The other teachers, professors, and students got after Galileo. They said, "That's crazy. The great Aristotle says otherwise. Prove what you're saying; convince us." He went to the top of the Leaning Tower of Pisa, he took a couple of weights; though they were of different sizes, they were of the same material. He dropped them, and they fell at the same rate of speed; they hit the ground at the same time. He convinced them beyond any doubt that they would fall at the same rate of speed.

Guess what they kept teaching at the University of Pisa? They kept teaching exactly what Aristotle had told them. Galileo had convinced. He had not persuaded.

How do you persuade? You persuade, as I did, with that series of nine questions a few minutes ago, not by telling people. But he convinced or you must convince by asking those questions. That's what I am saying.

In athletics, as I said earlier, you explore the opponent's weakness. In selling, you take their weakness and make it strong by selling the product. You persuade them to go ahead and get your goods and services, and that will strengthen their weaknesses.

Another point, which is critical in your sales career, has to do with the law of averages. You've been told this from time to time: If you make so many calls, you'll get so many appointments. If you make so many appointments, you'll make so many demonstrations, and with so many demonstrations, then you're going to end up with X number of sales.

I agree with the law of averages, but sometimes the law of averages will get you in trouble. For example, if I put one of my feet in a bucket of ice water and one of my feet in a bucket of boiling water, on the average, I am not going to be comfortable.

I believe you, as a salesperson, are exactly like this old farmer that I heard about. He did not want all the land, you might not want all the sales, but that farmer wants the land next to his. You don't want all the sales, but I'll bet you want the next one, don't you?

I want to ask you a question. Would you give me $100 for a product that you knew was worth only $25? I don't see any hands up. Suppose I used my three best bear-trap closes, then would you give me the $100 for the $25 value?

Suppose I explained that my wife and kids would suffer if you don't buy. Some of you softhearted or softheaded ones might go ahead and buy, but you're not going to build a career that way.

The sales point I want to make is this: when the prospect says no, you back up, because he won't change his mind. Let me say that again. When the prospect says no, he won't change his mind.

I know what you're thinking: "Wait a minute, Ziglar, every time I make a sale, they've already told me no, no, no." I don't doubt that for a moment. I asked the redhead to marry me, and she said no. I asked her the second time, no. Third time, no. Fourth time, no. Fifth time, no. Sixth time, she said OK, but she never changed her mind.

Please understand this, salespeople: when a prospect says no, before they can change their mind, they have to admit they were wrong, that they made a mistake.

Do you like admitting that you made a mistake? It's a tough thing to do. People don't do it, but let me tell you what they *will* do. They'll do exactly the same thing the redhead did. She made a new decision based on new information.

If you want to be professional in the world of selling, think of the prospect's mind as a pair of scales. When the value in the prospect's mind exceeds the price, you have a prospect, but as long as, in that prospect's mind, the price is $100 and the value is $25, you don't have a chance for a sale. Now you can't really change the price, but you can change the value.

That's the reason every close that you use should give additional information, so that with every close, that prospect is seeing more and more reasons for saying yes. When you get that value above the price, that is the point you will make a sale.

Even though the value is higher than that price in the prospect's mind, you still have to ask for the order. You still have to use professional skills. You still have to close the sale as a professional should.

You must not oversell. When I think of overselling, I think of the story of the Roman Catholic girl dating the Southern Baptist boy. After about the fifth date, she came home one evening, and she obviously was in trouble. I mean, mom looked at her and knew that her daughter was in love.

Mom said, "Now, daughter, you know us Catholics don't marry those Baptists, and those Baptists don't marry us Catholics. It's a losing proposition. I want you to terminate that relationship."

"Mom," the girl said, "it's too late. I've fallen in love. Can't we do something?"

The loving mother said, "Well, I'll tell you what let's do. Let's sell that boy on taking instruction. We'll make a good Catholic out of him, and when that happens, everything will be all right." So they went to work on the process, and it was an easy sale. That boy was really sold on the product. There was no question about that.

After he'd gone through the instruction, the wedding day was set, the announcements were sent out, the gifts starting coming in. Everything was all set. About a week before the wedding, the girl came in one night shedding those big tears, and said, "Mom, it's all off. Cancel the wedding. Send back the gifts. Call the priest. Tell our friends."

The mother said, "I'm puzzled. I can't understand it. I thought we had that boy sold on being a good Catholic."

The girl said, "Mom, that's the problem. We've oversold. He's going to be a priest."

Sell professionally, sell with the right skills, sell with the right intention, but don't oversell. I believe that's one of the most important secrets if you're going to build a career in the world of selling. Sell what it is, sell what it does, sell its true value, but don't exaggerate that value. When you oversell, you end up with a short career.

Selling Right to the Right People

Zig

For nearly forty years, it has been my privilege to be in as many sales situations as virtually anyone who ever called himself a salesman. I've sold everything from soap to securities, from sales training to you just name whatever the product might be. It has been my privilege to share the platform and learn from some of the greatest speakers and sales trainers our country has produced, and I've learned a great deal from them.

Experience is a great teacher, but it's important to realize we don't learn just from our own experience. We must learn from others' experience, and that's what we're doing next. We've brought together four successful salespeople who have a wide range of experiences and backgrounds, from communication systems to computers and typewriters, from personal recruiting to training and consulting services.

First, we have Phil Wynn, who's a classic example of how hard work in the sales industry will pay off. Phil began with our company as a part-time distributor of our books and tapes. He soon became the number-one distributor in sales and recruiting. As a result of his continued success, Phil was later offered the position of vice president of our video product sales team. Under his leadership, sales increased 195 percent in one year. Now Phil is vice president of all sales and marketing activities of the Zig Ziglar Corporation.

Then we have Jill Hammond, who received her BS from Texas Tech and her master's degree from Mississippi State. Jill has established herself as a top salesperson. Jill came to our company from a retail sales and personnel recruiting background. We like to think we recognize talent when we see it, and Jill certainly has made us look good.

As a telephone salesperson and customer service representative for the video training group, Jill became a top producer, setting records for the largest single sale ever recorded, and for the top sales week of any salesperson in our company. Jill now represents our company as a speaker and training consultant.

Janet Rush brings some vitally important insights to our discussion. Janet became a top sales leader in the communications industry, dealing with the national accounts of major corporations such as Execu-tone and Contel. Janet has been active in sales management and in the development of customer and client relation departments for companies within the communications industry. This experience has given her the expertise necessary to develop a top seminar on customer relations and telephone etiquette, which she delivers for Strawberry Communications, which is a subsidiary of the Zig Ziglar Corporation.

Bryan Flanagan began his fourteen-year career with IBM as a salesperson. IBM, recognizing Bryan's ability to lead others as well as to sell, placed him in the position of sales instructor for the company's national training center. In 1980, he earned the position of marketing manager of the largest branch of its office-products division.

In 1984, Bryan joined our company as marketing and development director in the area of corporate training. Since that time, Bryan has established himself as one of the top sales trainers in the country and has become the most highly scheduled speaker in our company. Why, he even speaks more than I do.

Here we will be addressing selling right to the right people.

There are some salespeople who will tell you that prospecting is the most important part of the process of selling. Others will say qualifying. Others will say presentation. Others will say closing. All will agree that until you have the prospect, you don't have a chance to do any of the others. The top professional salespeople always put prospecting first in their list of priorities. Our economic life depends on it.

I like to think of prospecting as the sin of the desert brought to life. The sin of the desert is simply this: an individual who knows where the water is and will not tell someone else—that's the sin of the desert. A customer who is sold on a product and who does not share that information by giving you the name of other prospects is guilty of the sin of the desert.

If you can persuade your customers of that, they will give you lots of prospects, but that's just one way of prospecting. I'd like to ask Phil Wynn for his definition of prospecting and what a prospect really is.

Phil

A prospect is the name of an individual and an introduction to that individual who can make a decision on my product or service. It doesn't matter whether I'm in real estate or an automobile dealership or whether I'm in computers or selling copiers, it's that individual who can make that decision.

Wayne

Yes, but you need to be sure that the people that you're talking to are prospects, not suspects.

Bryan

That really is the difference. What is the difference between a prospect and a suspect? To me a suspect is a name or a business, and it's filled with hope, but it's based on nothing else.

Wayne

I say a prospect has a need for your product, has a desire, and has the financial backing to make that decision, or else you're wasting your time talking to them.

Bryan

As Zig said earlier, that's vital, because I learned long ago that pressure selling is caused by a lack of prospects. When you're the last person I'm calling on that day, and my list is empty, you're the last name, and I'm in front of you. I have to make that sale. If I turn to the next day, and there's no prospects there, I'm going to put some pressure on me, unfortunately on you.

Zig

That's especially true if that gas tank is empty.

Jill

When's the best time to prospect? Whenever, wherever, however—all the time. It's not an 8:00 to 5:00 kind of thing.

Janet

I'm always thinking that someone needs my products, and I need to tell them. In a social situation after working hours—you may be at a social gathering, on a plane, in an airport—somebody is bound to ask you about what you do.

In my mind, that's prospecting, because if they give me an opportunity to share about what Janet does, and I find out what they do, you're immediately prospecting with people, whether you're sitting down at lunch, or whether you're sitting next to somebody in the theater. Everyone is a potential prospect.

Zig

Wherever you are, whatever you're doing, you are thinking prospecting. As long as you think of prospecting all the time, it's amazing how many times prospects will suddenly pop up out of the blue.

I'd like to add another thought: the last name you got, provided you had the proper amount of information on them, is the best prospect.

Why? It's not because they're better qualified; I'm assuming that you are qualifying them. They're the best because they're the last name you have, and you're the most excited about them. Something happens when you keep a superb prospect on file for six weeks. In some cases, nothing happens to the prospect, but a lot happens to our thinking about that prospect.

Here's a key: when you get that prospect, get busy and go see them.

Wayne

How do you go about doing that? What are some how-tos in prospecting?

Bryan

I ran across a fellow that was selling with the IBM Corporation. He had a COD prospecting method. He said that the C stood for *communication*. Every time you communicate with somebody, make those contacts, drive those prospects. O was for *observation*—whether it be listening to conversations in elevators or walking down the hall and looking at the listings in the marquee. The D stood for *dedication*. You need to be dedicated to it. As Jill said earlier, if you're in an 8:00 to 5:00 mentality and are not dedicated to prospecting on planes, airports, and social situations, then communication and observation alone won't do it. You have to be dedicated to driving prospects.

Phil

That is a very effective way of prospecting, but I found another one that I believe has done a tremendous amount for a lot of salespeople around the country. Some know it as *radiation prospecting*. Others call it *center of influence*.

It's like dropping a stone in a pond: you see it ripple out from the center. Radiation prospecting or center of influence means, I have an opportunity to present my product to one individual, then that individual introduces me to another, who introduces me to another. It radiates out through the whole circle of their acquaintances and friends until just from that one individual, I can have a number of different opportunities to talk to people about my product.

Janet

I had a friend pull me aside one day, and say, "Janet, why do you spend so much time selling everybody but the people you know best?" I stopped, and I thought. I said, "I didn't want you to think I was pushing my product on you." They said, "If you think it's good enough for all those strangers, why isn't good enough for your friends and your family?"

"That's pretty interesting," I said. "What would you like to buy?" Although the one group of people I seemed to back away from were friends and family, that was my strongest center of attention, where I would get good sales and good referrals. Many times we forget that circle of friends and family.

Bryan

We want to go out and make contacts and sell someone and use them as our center of influence. To me, Janet's point was that we need to think and say, "We have a center of influence. We can be a center of influence." Maybe the people that we go to church with, maybe the people that we socialize with, that we run into at different clubs, organizations, activities. We're a center of influence there.

Zig

A lot of times we get the impression that just because someone has given us a half dozen prospects they've run dry. I well remember one lady who had eleven dinner demonstrations for me, and each one was extraordinarily successful.

She did the demonstrations because she felt like she was doing her friends a favor, and she was a friend of mine. So she was introducing one group of friends to another friend, and so she had another motive in mind.

My major two points are these. Number one, the well is probably not dry from the person who's been supplying you leads. Number two, it is a social activity for a lot of people. If the product and services are good, they're pleased to introduce their other friends to what you're doing.

Wayne

Sometimes we sell a customer and then throw them aside. Even when we get a new product or a new option for the product they've already bought, we don't tend to think of our old customers. But you can go back to them: you have a new excitement, a new product or a new option, and you can turn to them.

Phil

When I was in the computer industry, I used to meet with the maintenance engineer and the service engineers about once a month and say, "Who have you been calling on that needs service on our equipment? What type of problems are they having? Do they need that piece of equipment replaced?"

Many times the serviceman would be talking to the librarian, and she'd say, "I'd like to have this new terminal over there in one section of the building." He'd come back and tell us. Or she'd say, "I'd like to have this new feature of software in our program," and he'd come back and tell us.

By sitting down with this guy once a month, I was able to find out the needs of many of our current customers, as well as of other prospects, and I could go out, visit with them, and make additional sales. So one referral type is to get acquainted with your service people and know what they're doing.

Bryan

Right here in the Dallas area, there are a lot of lead exchange clubs. When I was involved with a lead exchange club back in Baton Rouge, Louisiana way back when, it was a little bit less formal.

The lead clubs have changed over a period of time: they've gotten more formal and sophisticated. There are now sheets of paper. You must come prepared with five leads that you know and you've called on. You write them down on the form, and check off whether you want the salesperson to use you as a reference or not. There are fifteen or twenty people at a meeting, so you get fifteen or twenty sheets of paper, each with five names. You've got some leads there. That's at least a half-day's work.

Phil

We have a tremendous opportunity when we do that, because every one of us is in the sales environment all day long, and we're talking to people who need the products and services of our salespeople friends.

Janet

When I sold communications systems, I tied up with the person who was also selling communication, but a different service, in my area or field. When he sold something, it was natural for me to come and sell equipment. If I sold equipment, it was natural for them to have his service, so we did double legwork. We worked for different companies, but we networked between the two of us, and we actually doubled our sales in less than six months. I contributed that to him, and he contributed his doubling to me. That was the type of prospecting or referral that we used.

Phil

In referral prospecting, if I've just made a sale, I want to find out who the customer knows, but one of the first things I have to do is let them know why it's important to me.

Why am I going to ask for a referral? Many times I'd make a statement like this: "Bryan, you know, one of the most important tools that I have as a salesperson is a prospect. Today you've just taken that away from me, as you've become a customer. I need to replace that, so I need to be able to talk with someone else about my product and service."

Zig

When you're asking for prospects, the way you ask for them is of paramount importance. I've seen salespeople say, "I'd like to have five prospects. Would you fill these out for me?" Well, you put five prospect cards in front of some of your new customers, and they're going to panic. They can't think of one. If you get far more specific, and say, "I know that if your best friend, or a neighbor, you'd be willing to introduce them to me, wouldn't you?" they're going to smile and say, "Well, of course."

"I'm going to ask you to introduce me to your next-door neighbor or to a friend of yours by way of their name and address so that I might share your excitement about our product with them." I would specifically ask for a neighbor or a friend. I would ask for one. As soon as they've answered that, then I ask, who else do you consider a good friend that has an interest and need in whatever it is that we're selling? I'd go down the list one by one.

Some of the best prospectors that I've ever seen in the world of selling use prospecting as kind of a trial close. As they were getting down to the nitty-gritty of asking for the order, I've had a lot of instances where the prospect would say, "You know, old Charlie would sure be interested in this." I would instantly stop and write Charlie's name down.

Then I might get two or three more leads, and because he had given me the assurance that he was interested because he was getting Charlie involved, I would assume the sale and go ahead. I was prospecting and closing the sale all at the same time.

Jill

It wasn't so much that customers were unwilling to give me referrals. I've found that they're more than happy to give them to me. But they pulled a blank when I started asking for them. They just couldn't think of any right then. So they'd say, "Let me write them down and send them to you."

You know what happens. Things get in the way, so I found one of the best things I could do was to give them, for lack of a better word, mind joggers. Instead of just throwing it open and saying, "Who do you know who'd be interested?" I'd start talking about their centers of influence. "Do you play golf? Any of your golf buddies, bridge, whatever it was?" I would think of whatever mind joggers I could give them to start thinking of people. I found if I could give them mind joggers, their centers of influence, they would be more than willing to give me prospects.

Janet

I think a point here would be to make sure that you get back with your customer and let him know that you made the contact. Do it either do that by note, by card, or by a phone call: "I wanted to let you know that I did call your friend Mr. Jones, and we had a wonderful meeting, and I appreciate your interest also."

He's glad to hear that I did follow up on that or get some kind of feedback, because it's hard for me to go back and ask him to do it again. Otherwise he says, "By the way, did you ever call Mr. Jones?"

"Oh, I sure did. I did that a year ago," although you never let him know. So be courteous and let people know that you did use that referral or prospect.

Zig

I'd like to amen that, Janet. If you're going to build a career, that's an absolute must. It's good PR. It's building the base solidly. It really is important in that career.

Phil

I'd like to ask a question. You did a lot of work with IBM, and I'm sure that you learned to ask for referrals. Let's say the client gave you the names of three people—did you get any qualification from them?

Bryan

Yes. Specific to what Zig was saying earlier, I'm always trying to narrow that gap, to make sure to know, if I have five people, who I should call on first. Obviously, if you can qualify that referral, it makes it a lot easier for you as you do legwork. Say the customer has just bought your product. You're either installing it or delivering it or signing the order, and he's given you five or six names.

Ask that person to rate those for you. "Who should I call on first? Who has the most burning need for this?" That way you're getting qualifications from the referral.

Zig

I think it's most important there, though, that when you're getting the name, you don't do any qualifying at that point. You do not want to stifle the flow of names. You write those names down as fast and furiously as you can. Once the well has run dry on getting the names, then you go back to the top of that list and start getting specific information about each one. Now you're qualifying. Get the name first, qualify second.

Phil

Zig, a quick question. How do you handle the situation where a customer shows some hesitation in giving you a referral because they're a little bit concerned about using their name?

Zig

I make the presentation, and I simply leave the decision up to them. Probably the most unusual and most sincere compliment I've ever gotten, and the one I'm the most proud of, was when I was getting referrals once and I said to the lady, "As you know, all I do is demonstrate, and if they want what we're selling, that's fine. If they do not want what we're selling, that's fine too."

She said, "Yes, that certainly is true. You're really not much of a salesperson." That's so precious to me, because she had just written me a check for the biggest order the company had made. She had bought; I had not sold, and that's the dream circumstance to be in.

I would say to them, "I simply promise to represent you as a friend." When I went to that person, I would simply say, "I'm Zig Ziglar. Mrs. John B. Smith asked me to stop by and chat with you, and I promised her that I would. She said to me, 'I don't have any earthly idea whether or not they're going to be the least bit interested,' but she made me promise that I would come by and let you make that decision."

I've already covered a major objection when they say, "Well, I'm not interested."

"Well, that's what your friend said, but she was so excited. I really promised her I'd let you see this. Would now be the best time, or should I come back this evening or whenever?"

Phil

Say I'm a brand-new salesman. I've just gotten started in computers. I don't have anybody that I can get referrals from. What am I doing now? How do I get prospects? Where do I go from here?

Bryan

That could be the start of the observation part of the COD we talked about earlier—communicate, observe, and then dedicate. Sometimes we fail to look in our own backyard. In your office there are probably some user files, customer files, or a particular customer you may want to grow. You may want to take a customer and make that into an account and grow the account. They're right there, but too often we restrict ourselves by not looking around for some avenues to pursue, and they're right there in our own offices.

Phil

I'd like to hear a story that Zig has shared with us a time or two as it relates to prospecting whenever, wherever, and however. I think it has something to do with a patrolman.

Zig

I was coming in from Wilmington, North Carolina, one Saturday evening, and I was in somewhat of a hurry to get home. To tell you the truth, I was in a ridiculous hurry. I was driving over ninety miles an hour, and the long arm of the law got me.

He gave me a ticket, but we had a real nice visit. I maybe could have gotten away without a ticket. We really visited well and I persuaded him to let me stop in Monday when I was on my way back through and pay the fine. That was in the little town of Whiteville, North Carolina.

I went in to pay the fine on Monday, and as I was turning loose those $40, the thought occurred to me that this is not the way to increase your net worth. There was an attractive young lady there with a diamond on, so I said, "Do you mind if I ask you a question?"

She said, "No."

I said, "I noticed that you're wearing an engagement ring."

"Yes, I am."

"I also obviously noticed that you're working, and I'm just wondering if you're saving any money for your marriage while you're working."

She said, "Oh, yes, I am."

"Well," I said, "if there were something available which you will definitely need and use in your marriage, could you increase your savings by as much as $1 a month in order to take advantage of it?"

She said, "Oh, I sure could."

"If I had something out in the car that was absolutely beautiful that would fill a need that you will definitely need and use, would you be courteous enough to spend a few minutes looking at it?"

She kind of smiled and said, "I'm just fixing to go on break, so yes, I'd be glad to do that."

So I scooted to the car, brought my samples in, and put on a fast demonstration, and I asked the obligating questions. She was with this other lady, who also was on break. The other lady was married. I asked the obligating question, and she turned to the married lady and said, "What would you do?"

I cut in. I said, "Excuse me. Let me ask you a question. If you had known before you got married what you know now about raising a family and making house payments and all, and you had had an opportunity to get something like this before you got married, would you have done it?"

"I sure would," she said.

I turned to the young lady who was getting married and said, "That's what you want to do, isn't it?"

She said, "Yes, I do."

I wrote the order, and when I finished writing it, I said to the other one, "Ten years ago, you didn't have this opportunity, and I'm certain you don't want to miss it this time, do you?"

"No, I don't," she said.

I wrote both of those orders, and on the way out of town, I saw that same highway patrolman. This time I stopped him, thanked him for the ticket, and told him what I had done. So, as you say, Phil, you prospect where you are. That's really the way to do it.

Phil

But that's not a method you'd recommend to all of us, would you?

Zig

I think you can get prospects for less than $40, and you don't have to go ninety miles an hour to get one, but I do think you need to be aware at all times.

Phil

When I was selling training materials in Utah, I used a method that I learned to call the eagle-eye method. I used to carry a tape recorder right on the car seat beside me. As I would drive from one call to another, drive by a building that looked like it might have a company in there that could use our material, I would just record into my recorder the name of the company and the location.

When I got home, I would give that to my daughter, who was working with me, and she would take the information and put it on a 3 x 5 card, look it up in the telephone directory, get the phone number, call the company, get the name of the president and how many people they had and a few other qualifying items of information. She'd set aside the ones that were not qualified and would me give just the ones that were qualified.

I would then call them up, set an appointment, and go out and see them. That's what I called eagle-eye prospecting—always looking for the prospect in whatever situation.

There's a source in the library that a lot of people are not aware of called *Contacts Influential.* You can go into the library, pick up a copy, and get the names of organizations listed by street. So if you're doing what some people call cold calling—I'd prefer to call it warm prospecting—you walk down the street and you know the names of every business on that street. It also gives you the CEO, so you have a little more information when you walk in the door than if you just walked in cold.

As a matter of fact, Bryan, I think you mentioned one time that the library has a lot of other sources, business lists, and I believe you even mentioned the Chamber of Commerce.

Bryan

The Chamber of Commerce has lists. So does the Better Business Bureau. Again, we need to put our thinking caps on, be creative, and seek out those organizations that have done a lot of the legwork for you. The courthouse has lists of new businesses opening. There are permits being filed, different buildings going up, leases, etc. Too often, though, we want it a little easier than to go into that library. If that's the case, if you want to work easy, you'll get paid easy.

Zig

The newspaper announces new births, and if you sell products that are related to that or if it indicates there might be an additional need for insurance, anything of that nature, you may have some leads. Prospects are everywhere, but we need to have that prospecting awareness.

Phil

I think it goes back to the comment I've heard Zig make before about the hardest work—what is it you say, Zig?

Zig

The best-paying hard work in the world is the world of selling. The poorest-paying easy work in the world is the world of selling. The salesperson who is sold on what they're doing never thinks of it as work.

I have a friend who always says, "I'm going out to play today, and I'm going to play hard. I'm going to play with a lot of different people." He does literally refer to it as play. That's important.

This might not be applicable, but I'd like to bring this thought out. In the last fifteen years, I've been very fortunate inasmuch as I have not had to solicit a speaking engagement. I believe one reason is, every time I make a presentation, I give it my very best shot. As I sat here listening to each one of you, I thought, "Well, won't that work for salespeople?" If each salesperson gives it the best shot, keeps it professional all the way, maintains all of their promises, won't their customers be doing what my customers are doing, sending them to other people to share the good news about their good products and services?

I'd like to wrap this up with this incident, which we talked about a great deal within our company. When I entered the world of selling, we were knocking on doors. I was in the cookware business. A lot of people still knock on doors for prospects, some in residences, and some in businesses.

I knocked on doors every day for ten days. I was getting absolutely nowhere. In ten days, incredibly enough, I could not even persuade anybody to let me in the house to tell my story, and yet I kept knocking on those doors.

I so well remember that August day in Columbia, South Carolina. There were two long city blocks. It was Idalia Drive. I was headed for Divine Street. In my mind I said, "If I don't at least get in somebody's house, I am going to quit this business." Down the street I went, doing my best to persuade people to let me show them what we had to offer.

I knocked on the next to last house in the block. A Mrs. B.C. Dickert, who was an older lady, came to the door. I told her my little story. She said, "Well, it sounds like something my brother and his wife, Mr. and Mrs. J.O. Freeman, next door would be interested in. Why don't you go see them? And if they decide to look, tell them to call me."

I ran next door. That was the first ray of hope, the first bright bit of sunshine I'd encountered. I knocked on the door. Mrs. Freeman was there. I told her a little story. She said, "Why don't you come back this evening?"

I got back that evening, and they called Mrs. Dickert over. I made the presentation, and Mr. and Mrs. Freeman bought a set of the cookware. It was set number 541. It sold for $61.45, and the down payment was $16.45. Oh, how well I remember it.

I was so elated, I sat there basking in the glory. At long last, I had a sale. I was just sitting there grinning, and then Mr. Freeman said, "Mr. Ziglar, I believe if you ask her to, Mrs. Dickert might buy a set of this cookware."

So I said, "Well, what about it, Mrs. Dickert?"

"I don't have my money with me," she said.

Very diplomatically, I said, "Well, shoot. You just live next door. Go get it."

"I just think I'll do that," and she went next door, got her checkbook, and came back, and I made that sale.

I cannot begin to tell you how excited I was. I've thought about that so many times. I was two houses away from ending my career. I made a decision that day that I would not ever again stake my career on what somebody else might do. I decided *I* would make the decision.

But there's a major point I want to make. Sometimes you do have to suck it up and tough it out and hang in there, but in today's world there are an awful lot of prospects out there, and if you're selling a good product at a fair price and you really believe in it, if you'll use the principles we've been sharing with you, I believe you can find all of the prospects you want.

CHAPTER 5

The Effective Use of the Phone in Sales

Zig

In 1982, the publishing company McGraw-Hill did an extensive study of 605 companies in America. They discovered it cost $178 to make an average sales call. That included airfare, transportation through automobile, meals, motel, things of that nature, salary for the salesperson. That's a lot of money. It took an average of 5.2 calls to make a sale. So the quality of the prospect is obviously extremely important.

I have a good friend who is an extraordinarily successful salesperson. To demonstrate the importance of having the prospect qualified, he does group selling. He puts on a demonstration in front of a group of people generally with the owner or the manager present. If the owner or manager is present, over a lifetime in his career of sales, he's closed an average of 45 percent every time. If the decision maker is not present, his closing ratio is 8 percent.

In a nutshell, he's five times as likely to sell if the decision maker is there. Is it important to qualify your prospects? You draw your conclusions. For me, that's very, very clear. I hope it is for you.

Bryan, I know I wouldn't get any argument out of you at all that quality prospects, qualified prospects, if you will, are the key to success in selling.

Bryan

For certain, Zig. If it's costing $178 for that call, it's vital that you sell right to the right person. Too often, though, it's not just the young salespeople going out there and calling on the wrong person. Sometimes the experienced reps get excited about a new product or a modified product, and they get so excited that they go out there and give their entire presentation to the wrong person.

We really do have to make sure that we're presenting to the right prospect. The question then is, what is a qualified prospect?

Phil

I really appreciate that figure that Zig threw out: we can close five times more if they're qualified than if they're nonqualified. So, for me, I'd love to see if they have a need for our product. That would be number one.

Number two would be, are they financially able to meet that need? Number three, do they really have a burning desire to meet that need, or is it a need that's just lying there? Those are three criteria that I would put together to say this is a qualified prospect.

Bryan

There we're assuming, of course, that this is the person within the organization that is authorized to make that decision. With those three criteria that you've established, that would be the right prospect then.

Janet

You have to ask, "Are you the person who is in charge of making this decision? Once you decide that you like my product, will you be the one to actually purchase it?" If he says no, you're in front of the wrong audience. Find the right person to talk to.

We can ask the customer very politely if he is responsible in that area. If not, who is? Or even call on the phone and say, "Who's in charge of operations that would be purchasing this type of equipment?"

Phil

In our company, we have a whole series of questions that we ask to determine whether or not we have a qualified prospect. We go down through that series so that our salespeople don't go out and spend that prospect's time, or our time, making a presentation when there is no opportunity of involving them in our product. I think you made a good point there, Janet. We can find out if they're the decision maker by simply asking and finding out.

Zig

Since I'm part of the process you were talking about, Phil, I'm obviously very interested in it. When I'm group prospecting during some of my presentations, I will always ask the audience, "How many of you are decision makers in your company?" When the hands go up, I say, "Here's what our offer is. If you have an interest in it, and you are a decision maker, give us your card and write the word *video* on it."

That does a couple of things. It indicates their interest, but then we can see their card, and we find out very quickly if they are the decision maker or not.

Phil

It's a whole lot easier to talk to those that really are the decision makers and are interested in building their company than it is to those who are not.

Janet, a minute ago you talked about finding out who the decision maker is. What do we do when we find out we find out we *don't* have a person who's in the decision-making position? How do we get to the next step? What's your experience been in that area?

Janet

Once I ask, then I usually proceed to take that person with me to introduce me to the next person who's going to be the decision maker.

It brought up a point to me. Many times I've presented in front of a person who was delegated the responsibility of searching out the proper product or vendor. Once they made the decision to go with me, I would say, "Who else is going to see this presentation? Who else do I really have to talk to?" which meant I had to go before a board of directors, a board of trustees, a hospital board, because there was still one final sale to make. This was going to be to a group of people, and I wanted to make sure the person who was sold he went with me to make that next presentation. Especially in large companies that are spending lots of money, I knew that I had probably more than one decision maker that I would have to sell.

Bryan

It's also important to differentiate between the decision maker and the influencers. Oftentimes we will step over that influencer to go to the decision maker. We leave, and we're outsold by someone internal because we didn't treat the influencer right.

When I was selling small systems with IBM—word-processing equipment—often the decision maker would delegate. The influencer would be using it, so he or she would study it, gain all the information. You would make an initial presentation through that person.

Sometimes you would take it to the decision maker together. Sometimes you weren't allowed to. Often we did not take advantage of using that influence, and that's difficult.

I also learned early the hard way, through losing money, that you never let anyone else sell for you. Don't say, "I can train this person enough on my equipment and give him or her the feature benefits so that that person can go sell the decision maker." It can't be done. Don't let anyone sell for you. Go with that person. Put your arm around him, pat him on the head, go in there together, and get it done.

Zig

I think what you're saying is extraordinarily important, Bryan, because there is a vast difference in understanding something well enough to *buy* it versus understanding something well enough to *sell* it, and that's exactly what you're saying. If all salespeople understood that, they would take the same approach. Man, I don't want anybody else selling for me.

I was just thinking of the Pilgrims. You remember when Myles Standish sent John Alden to talk to the pretty girl? You know what happened as a result of that: "Speak for yourself, John," and the rest of it is history. Nobody else is going to represent your interests as well as you can.

Phil

Fortunately for all of us, qualifying is a skill. In other words, we can learn it. So let's take a few moments and brainstorm qualifying. Let's see if we can come up with a series of steps that would help us to be able to qualify prospects. What would be some of the first things we would think about, some of the first questions we would ask?

Jill

You go back to your first definition of a qualified prospect. One of the conditions is, do they have a need? The first thing I have to find out is, do you have a need for my product, or can I create a need for my product?

Janet

Sometimes it's what do they have now that I'm going to either replace or bring to them that is new? So I want to make sure that I know what they have at the present. That shows my knowledge and interest in their company.

Phil

Perhaps even, Janet, what do they like about what they have now? What features do they like about the product that they already have?

Janet

The point there is never to sell down what they already have. Many times the salesperson is so excited about that new product that he will tend to talk down what someone has bought previously. When you say that, you're saying to the person, "Well, you didn't have enough sense. Why on earth did you buy that?" That's the underlying statement.

Instead you're going to build up to your purchaser what he's previously bought. That's his intelligence. He made that decision, and I'm going to make him feel important about making that decision, but I have something that could be better for him.

Bryan

That point was brought out very well with the IBM Corporation for many years. I don't know if it still goes on there or not, but for the fourteen years I was with IBM, two times a year I signed an agreement stating that I would never disparage the competition.

If I wanted to lose my job, that was the fastest way to do it. You could misquote occasionally. You could miss appointments occasionally. But if you disparaged or talked down the competition, that was the fastest way to lose your job, because that's not the way to compete.

If we're going out and there are some competitors, we have to have enough knowledge to find out if in fact the prospect has Brand 102.

If I have that competitive knowledge, then perhaps I know about how this person uses the product. I have a head start, rather than going out there completely blind, not knowing anything, and then having to ask those replacement-selling questions: What do you have? What do you like about it? If you could wave your magic wand, what would you replace? Those are the criteria that I'm trying to draw out so that I can qualify not only the prospect, but also the product.

Zig

You're dealing with one of the oldest psychological principles known, and that is the best way to sell a prospect a new product is to make them happy with the old product. That gives them confidence that they have the ability to make good decisions. If you question their judgment and ability to make a good decision earlier, then you entertain doubt in their mind on this one. If you say, "You really were taken," then in essence they're going to say, "Yes, that fellow got to me, but you are not." So IBM has a marvelous policy there. Smart.

Janet

Also don't assume that your customer knows all about the product he's picking out. In the communications industry, I found that many times someone had been delegated that responsibility, and they were really seeking knowledge from me. My competition would just assume that this particular person knew all about communication systems when in fact he knew absolutely nothing. He was looking for a salesperson to help him, to educate him, and not just automatically assume that he had all this knowledge. So as we're qualifying, we're very careful about using slang words that are used in your industry, not in theirs.

Phil

One other point that we skipped over when we were talking about defining the need is to understand the environment that our customer is operating in, to understand the type of business they're in, to understand how long they've been in business and exactly what they do. When we ask questions, we try to find out what the background of the company is, and that helps us to zero in on the need.

Bryan

That nails down the need. From that need, you have to have an awareness. Once you have the awareness, it's a little easier to present something to the prospect. Just as importantly, you have to gather all the criteria, all the information.

The prospect, whether he's qualified or not, needs to have an awareness. If he's sitting there waiting for you to come in his office, he does not know he has a need, so by asking the questions, getting those criteria, you're becoming aware, but you really have to show the awareness to the prospect.

Janet

Here's a question I used to ask. It's very blunt: "If you could design this phone system, what would you have it do that would be ideal? If you had the ideal product, what would it do?" I can tell you right away, they'll list ten or fifteen things. "I'd like for it to do this and this," and immediately, I know exactly how I'm going to sell my product, because he's told me exactly what he would like if he could have an ideal system in his office.

Phil

Zig, you say that if you ask the right question, the prospect will tell you how to sell him. When you ask that question, you find out what that need is, you know exactly what points to make in your sales presentation, and the prospect will sell himself.

Zig

Yes, I think also, Phil, we need to clearly understand that prospecting and qualifying are important, but sometimes we need to be very careful in our judgment.

I recall that when my youngest daughter graduated from high school, one of our commitments to her was to get her a new car. We went down to get the new car, and I want to stress a couple of things.

I was working that day, so I was dressed approximately as I am at this moment. Now my daughter had not been to bed the night before. She'd been getting dressed. Listen, this was her first new car. You're talking about dress fit to kill. As we'd say down home, she had on her Sunday-go-to-meeting best. I drive a nice car.

We pulled up in front of the dealership. A young salesman greeted us as we walked in, and though we gave indications of being reasonably affluent, he offered charity. "Can I help you?" I don't believe in playing games, especially when I'm in a hurry, so I said, "My daughter just graduated from high school, and we're looking for her a new car."

He looked right at me and said, "If you see anything you like, let me know," and I promise you, he turned around and walked away. Now I don't know what constitutes a good automobile prospect, but here I am a daddy with his daughter who just graduated from high school. He's promised her a car, publicly announces he's going to buy it, possibly or probably has the money to do it. I don't know how much more qualification you have to have before you merit a sales presentation.

We went to the next dealership, and the response and reception were almost exactly the same except even worse. That salesman had BO. We went to the third dealership—almost as bad, and I'm not just after automobile salespeople. If you notice, I started the whole series talking about an extraordinary professional automobile salesman.

We went to the fourth dealership and got lucky, because my daughter had dated the salesman. We had an in with that dealership. We were able to buy the car, and it didn't take us but a few minutes to do it. I thought to myself how unfortunate it is that we have to have a connection in order to make a purchase.

In case you think I'm just trying to entertain you, let me nail it down with what the Sales and Marketing Executives Club found. They found that the number-one reason for failure among salespeople was the fact that they prejudged the prospect as to whether they were going to buy or not.

Don't misunderstand what I just said. First of all, you do qualify them. Then you put them on trial, and if they are qualified, you find them guilty of being a purchaser. Don't decide that even though they're qualified, they're not going to buy. Once you have them as a qualified prospect, give them your absolute best shot.

Jill

There is nothing more aggravating than that. I had that same situation with a time-share, and the man prejudged that I wasn't going to buy. Yet we both had to sit through an hour of him talking. By every indication he thought, "She's not going to buy, she's not going to buy." So I started thinking, "I'm not going to buy, I'm not going to buy." By prejudging that, you do a real disservice to the consumer.

Janet

I think about how many times I've had customers or sales presentations, and I thought, "Boy, this one's a winner. I know he's going to buy," and he doesn't buy. And there's the one over here that I spent little time on and, I thought, had no chance in the world. That's the one that bought from me. I thought, "There I go." I was assuming this one would, this one wouldn't. Many times we're surprised by salespeople, because that's exactly what happens to us.

Phil

Going back to a point that we touched on earlier: who is the decision maker, and then who in addition to yourself will be involved in making this decision?

In our training program, many times when we go into an office, we talk maybe to one, two, or three decision makers. Invariably we find that if we're only able to talk to one of them, then our chances of involving them in our product are much slimmer. If we can get all three or four of them together, we have the opportunity to close that sale.

Janet

I've seen many a salesperson go in and beg for the presentation, or get the presentation and say, "If all of you are busy, I'll see you today, and I'll see you tomorrow, and I'll see you the next day and the next day." He's willing to make presentations separately to all four, which I think is a lot of time, when if he'd ask when is the best time that he can get them together, his chance of closing is much higher.

Many times, we feel that we don't want to ask them for their time. They're very busy, but the management team admires that: here's somebody that doesn't want to waste everyone's time four times. We're going to do it one time, and that's the appointment that I will get.

Zig

To hitchhike on what you said a moment ago, if the salesperson goes and makes those four presentations, the message they communicate is that my time is not important. Yours is the only one that is, and the first thing you know, that company will have no interest in dealing with that salesperson. They will treat them very shabbily and will abuse that person.

The one who gets all four of the people together, they will respect that individual more, and people don't buy from people they don't respect. They just don't.

Janet

Zig's been talking a lot about going door-to-door, and I think that's fabulous, but now we rarely have the time to actually go door-to-door in making our presentations, so we use the next best thing, which is the telephone. I'd like to open it up to see how each of you use the telephone in qualifying people. It's an important tool we use, and I find that most people do not know how to use it.

Phil

I believe the primary problem is that a lot of salespeople, for whatever reason, are afraid of the telephone. I don't quite understand why. I enjoy operating on a telephone as much as I do face-to-face. Why do you think salespeople are afraid to reach out and use that tool to help them set appointments?

Zig

I might not know all the reasons why they're afraid of it, but to emphasize what you're saying, we did a little study, and as nearly as we can figure, there have been 100 million salespeople who have used the telephone. They have made billions of telephone calls, and our latest study reveals that never in history has a single salesperson lost their life while trying to get an appointment via the telephone.

So of all the things we do, that easily rates as the safest one of them all. Now, Janet, why are they afraid to use that telephone?

Janet

Many times salespeople will say, "I don't want to make that presentation on the phone. I have to see them eye-to-eye." I'm saying you don't have to make the presentation on the phone. I want you to get the appointment. The use of the phone is basically to get the appointment, not give them all the information, because if you do, most likely you won't get the appointment.

Basically the phone is to get appointments, to get in to see people, and that's how it needs to be used rather than for selling.

Jill

So you're saying we need to know what we're selling at each stage of the selling process.

Janet

Right. You plan your calls. The best and most effective people on the phone are the people who plan calls. What am I going to say? Who am I going to talk to? Who am I going to ask for? I'm going to make it short and brief and get on to the next one.

How long would it take you to make twenty-five cold calls door-to-door versus twenty-five phone calls?

Phil

Since I used to make calls door-to-door, my goal was to talk to twenty people a day, and banging on twenty doors a day. It takes a whole lot less time to get on that telephone and set those appointments, Janet.

I encourage any salesperson to use that tool. The best way to begin to use it, in my opinion, is to reach out and pick it up. That's a very simple solution, very common sense, but as Zig has taught us so many times, logic won't change an emotion, but action will. The action of reaching out, picking it up, and beginning to use it begins to take away that fear.

Bryan

We need to have goals when we start doing that. If, in fact, we're going to spend two hours this morning prospecting, two hours qualifying, two hours setting up appointments, let's have those goals outlined for us, because in the first thirty minutes we need to know where we stand. Am I above my goal, below my goal? Get me some direction as I'm on that phone calling and trying to generate appointments.

If we have a direction, it's a little easier. We understand why we're doing it. Too often we don't. That's one thing that restricts us as salespeople from using that phone.

Zig

To combine what the two of you are saying, in all of the years I made telephone appointments, and in all of the years I knocked on doors, I never reached the point where I enjoyed knocking on that first door or making that first telephone call.

My solution—and the only reason I believe I survived—was the fact that I made an appointment with myself that at precisely the same time every day, I would either be knocking on that door or making that first phone call, regardless of what else took place. As Phil said, you make the telephone call by picking it up, and you start dialing.

A funny thing. After about the third call, I started having fun with it, but if I had not made the first one, I would not have been having fun by the third one.

Janet

Rejection is hard on the phone, but I'd rather have rejection on the phone than in person any day.

Bryan

We have to separate rejection from refusal. They may not be buying you over the phone or in person, but that really is refusing to listen to you, to see you. They're not personally rejecting you.

Too often, we don't understand that, and we think, "Poor, poor, pitiful me." There's only a handful of people that know you well enough to reject you personally, and those are your closest associates, friends, family. The rest of the people are saying, "No, I don't choose to listen to you." That's a business refusal, not a personal rejection.

Zig

One of the most important assignments, and sometimes one of the toughest, is getting to the decision maker through the guardian of the gate. Sometimes that's an administrative assistant, sometimes it's a secretary. Phil, how do you go about doing that?

Phil

One of the first things we have to think about is how we look at that administrative assistant or secretary. Are they a block, or are they an assistant to me? So the first point is, how am I going to treat that individual?

I say treat them kindly. Find out what their name is and what they do. Treat them in a way that they know that they're an asset to us, and they're going to help us get to that busy decision maker.

Bryan

They're oftentimes the influencer within that account. They will influence the decision maker, sometimes before you get there. If you set an appointment through this person, if you follow Phil's directions and you've made them feel important, and you understand that they're a person, not a "screener" or a "gatekeeper," then perhaps they can tell the decision maker, "Hey, you're going to look forward to this call. This person has his or her act together. The presentation will be good. You need to talk to these people."

Phil

Janet, you've made a point in earlier discussions about how you note the secretary's name down, and I believe the next time you call, you're certain that you ask for that person by name.

Janet

You bet. In my old book, next to my customer's name, I always have the name of the secretary who will answer the phone. As soon as they pick up the phone, I'll say, "Hi, Lucy. This is Janet with Strawberry."

I do not hesitate. Rather than saying, "May I speak with Mr. Jones?" I immediately give my name and my company. I know the question I'm going to get: "Who's calling? What is this in reference to?" If you sound like you're very familiar with them, you have a better chance of getting through.

Phil

You made another point, which I'd like to elaborate on. When you say, "Hi, Lucy. This is Janet with Strawberry. May I speak to—" instead of "Mister," say, "May I speak to Ed? Is he in, please?" I always use the first name and ask the question, "Is he in, please?" The implication is a personal relationship with that individual, which I do want to develop as I'm sharing with him about our product or our service.

Janet

Sometimes it would help us not to ask a lot of questions on the phone when we're trying to get to that person. We'll call and say, "What do they do, and what are they in charge of?" It's obvious that we haven't done our homework, and that we're going to be selling something. Consequently, we're not going to get through. So be careful about the number of questions you ask of the person who picks up that phone.

Phil

So point number one is, do your homework. Another point is, control the conversation. In other words, we have to get them to help us to get to the appropriate individual.

Zig

When you go about asking for getting on through, Janet, specifically what words do you say to the secretary you've called?

Janet

If I know the person's name, I simply say, "Lucy, this is Janet Sue with Strawberry Communications. I'd like to speak with Ed." That's exactly how I say it. Very short, very concise.

Zig

What if she says, "What is this about?" or "What's the purpose of the call?" In other words, even though she recognizes the name, she's not quite ready to let you through. Suppose she says, "He's busy now" or "What's the call specifically about?" What would you say?

Janet

I would tell her, "I'm going to speak with Mr. Jones or with Ed regarding a seminar that's coming to his city next week or in a month."

Bryan

Sometimes we lose sight of the fact that when we're talking with the influencer, we need to sell the influencer. When we talk to the decision maker, we have what they call a general benefits statement or a direct benefits statement, such as "This involves Ed saving 15 percent on his whatever cost. This involves increasing his productivity by 12 percent. This involves a training course that would help his salespeople be better organized." That way the influencer cannot make decisions on salespeople usually.

If you're talking to the vice president of sales, that's his or her department. The influencer doesn't make that decision. If, in fact, you give that statement and mentally say to the influencer, "This has to go to his or level. You better put them through," the general benefit statement and the definite benefit statement would definitely help.

Phil

Another point is that in any selling situation, there will be objections raised. We have to have already planned for those objections and decided what we're going to say, and be able to respond over the phone.

Janet

Most times they'll say, "He's on the phone," or "She's on the phone. She's busy. She's in a meeting." Those are the three top answers we get. I simply say, "What is the best time for me to call back to reach them?" Ask the question so they can say, "At the end of the day, at noon, in an hour, two hours," and then make that call again at that time.

The good thing about that is that if they say between 1:00 and 3:00, and you make it back, Lucy feels some responsibility in getting you through, because her word's on the line. She's told you he's going to be there between 1:00 and 3:00. There's a sense of responsibility to let you on through.

Phil

If I'm having difficulty getting through to an individual, and we're playing telephone tag back and forth, I use the question "What time does he come into the office in the morning?" because usually the first half hour to forty-five minutes in the morning is not that hectic. If I know what time that individual's coming in, I'll plan my call early in the morning, when I can catch him.

Janet

I found that decision makers usually answer their own phones very early in the morning. If I call them by 7:00 or 7:30, there's no one else there to answer the phone, and many times they'll answer themselves. I have the decision maker on the phone before the day even begins. I used to make most of my calls between 7:00 and 8:00.

What are some specific skills that any of you might use in using the phone, Jill? You use the phone all day long. What do you do?

Jill

I think one of the first things that you need to do is show enthusiasm to your customers. You see, face-to-face you'd be there, you'd be smiling, you'd be happy, you'd be enthusiastic about your product.

You can do that over the phone with your voice. Put a smile in your voice, have your personality shine through the phone. Let them know a little bit about you. I think your voice can create a lot of the enthusiasm that you lose when you don't have that face-to-face contact.

Bryan

I've seen different sales reps even have mirrors in the office, so they can see how they look to that customer, although the customer obviously can't see them. It helps cement the fact that you're talking to a person rather than a prospect.

A lot of folks stand up at their desks to speak. Now I've tried that occasionally, and it's getting more comfortable for me, and I think it's more comfortable for my voice. Sometimes you get like that. You get kind of monotone. You stand up and have a little bit more enthusiasm, or at least a little bit more inflection and modulation to your voice, which is important.

And although you need to have a watch or a clock, a stopwatch, in front of you, you also need to have a basic outline if you do not use a totally planned presentation, because if you're not careful, you will end up wandering and spending a lot of time and wasting time and money in the process. I believe that's extremely significant.

I too like to stand up when I'm using the telephone if it's a business call. If I'm chatting and visiting, I rear back, I sit down, I might put my leg up on the table or the desk. But one thing I always do in a phone call is this: if I'm going to be more than three minutes, I ask, "Have I caught you at a good time?" or "Would it better if I tried again in a few minutes at a more convenient time?"

If they give me the assurance that they have a couple of minutes, then I go ahead, but if they say, "No, this really is a bad time," you cannot sell the appointment if they have something else on their mind at that moment.

Janet

Do you know how many times I've had salespeople on the phone say that to me, and I'll say, "No, this isn't a good time," and they continue with their spiel? I said, "No, this isn't—" I say that three times before they get the message because they weren't listening to me when I said no. They just continued, and of course it's real hard for me to get back into it with them at a later date. I think if they listen to me, I would have probably told them, "Call me back at a better time."

Phil

I like what Zig just said. Several years ago when I was using the telephone extensively to make appointments, I would ask that same basic question: "Do you have a few moments we can talk?" They'd say, "Well, I don't, but go ahead and tell me what you're calling about."

I refused to tell them what I was calling about, because I didn't have enough time to give my presentation, and they'd make a snap judgment, a snap decision. I would come back and say, "I really don't have enough time to give you a full presentation. It wouldn't be fair to you or to me. When is a good time for me to call you back?"

Zig

Say, "This is too important for you to make a decision based on inaccurate or incomplete information for you. I'd be pleased to get back to you," and then you set the appointment for the proper time.

Bryan

That's part of the qualification process. You have to qualify if it's the right time to make the presentation. If you go to somebody's office, it's the same way.

You're standing out in the lobby, and they come and want you to give the presentation. But that is not the time to give a presentation. That is not the qualified prospect at that time.

The same is true over the phone, and you can tell. Someone will be putting the phone down and shuffling through papers—all this noise in the background. It's not the right time. They're not honing in on you at all.

Janet

They tell us that the first three to five seconds set the entire stage, mood, and atmosphere of your relationship with someone on the phone. So I say to myself, "I have three seconds to make that impression." Three seconds is real quick, so we want to remember that as we're dealing with people on the phone.

Phil

I'd like to bring us back to a few seconds prior to that call. I read several years ago in a book about a gentleman. On every call that he was making, as he began to walk in the door, he would reach out, put his hand on the doorknob, and stop. He would visualize in his mind a successful sales presentation.

In his mind he would visualize the prospect signing the order, and then he'd open the door and walk in. I'm suggesting that as I reach for that phone, I stop. I visualize success. I expect success. I expect the appointment, and I pick up the phone and make the call.

Zig

Along those same lines, I think it's important to understand that we do get paid on every single call we make, regardless of what happens. We all have an average. Some of them are higher than others, but every time we dial that number, whether anyone answers it or not or whether the line is busy or whether we do or don't get through or whether we do or don't get the appointment, we definitely are paid for that call. We have a certain amount that we're paid for it. We need to figure that out and put three silver dollars or fifteen silver dollars right in front of us. Whatever the amount is, use real money. Look at it, and when you pick up the telephone, think "Boy, look what I'm going to get when I pick that telephone up." I guarantee that helps to inspire.

A second step you could take is put the most moving testimonial letter you have, from people who benefited enormously from your goods or services, right in front of you. You pick up the telephone and say, "Boy, maybe this is the one who will have even more benefits than this one."

Phil

I'm happy to hear you make that point, because Jim Savage in our own company has talked with some of his telephone people about doing that, and I have seen some of those testimonial letters in their offices. When you read that letter, it really inspires you to go ahead and handle each one of those calls.

Jill

Another specific how-to is this: If you work out of your office at home, we tend to say, "I'm at home, nobody can see me. I'll wear jeans and be comfortable." Just like you have a posture for a casual call, and you have a posture for a business call, you need to be dressed for business. Whether you ever step out of your house or not, if you're working out of your home and calling, you need to be dressed for business, because you hear the difference in your voice.

Janet

I will attest to that, because I took a group of people who came to work every day in T-shirts and jeans, and I asked them, "Is the power of dress important on the phone?" Their comment was, "No, nobody sees me."

I asked them to dress in business attire for two weeks and come to work. I cannot tell you the difference in the appointments they got, the way they projected themselves on the phone, their personalities, their professionalism, the way people viewed them, even in the office. But the image they had was, "I'm just talking on the phone, I don't need to do that."

I support the idea that dress is important even over the phone.

Here's a question I ask myself when I hang up. I say, "Did that person at least like me after he got through talking me?" If I can get a yes, or I feel they did, I feel I had a successful call.

Zig

In other words, you're selling successfully on every call when you at least accomplish that objective, and that really prepares you to be more effective on the next call that you make. That's a very neat idea.

We could get carried away and spend a couple of hours on this subject, but understand that we are attempting to keep a promise that we made to you when you invested in what we're now doing. We said, "We won't make a promise without a plan. We won't tell you what you ought to do unless we share with you how to do it."

I hope you agree with me that these few minutes we've had together on this concept of qualifying and using the telephone is something you can use to further your career in selling. When you're selling right to the right people, it sure is fun.

6

CHAPTER

Preparing Successful Sales Presentations

Zig

In days gone past, a wise person said, "People don't plan to fail, they just fail to plan." I believe that would be applicable in the world of selling. If you're going to sell right to the right people—and that is the basic game plan—then obviously you have to have a plan to do it.

Is a plan important? Let me give you a little analogy. In the National Football League, during the last two minutes of the first half and the last two minutes of the game, more points are scored than during any other 30 percent of the entire game. That's because they have a specific game plan they follow.

A lot of salespeople miss sales because they do not have a specific plan of action. I'm here to tell you that a prospect is too precious to waste on an unplanned call. It's too expensive to see them if we do not have a plan which will enable us to present our goods, our products, our services in the most marketable manner.

So let's look at a plan for doing exactly that. Phil, when we talk about plans, you're one of the most careful planners I know, so give us some help on this one, please.

Phil

To me, Zig, one of the most important aspects of our entire presentation is the presentation itself. Thinking through the benefits, thinking through the product, thinking through the values that we want to communicate to our prospect. If I don't plan that presentation and write it out concisely and memorize it and get to the point where it's reflexive, I'm not able to always present the same picture to each prospect.

You have told us many times that we should always make as good a presentation at the end of the day as we make at the beginning, and I think we can only do that if we have a planned, organized presentation.

Bryan

As has been said in many areas—and selling is no exception—preparation compensates for lack of talent. If we have that structure, that plan going out there, we know how to respond to the prospect's questions or objections. Then we have a chance. But if we fail to plan, the chances are slim.

Jill

I don't think we use our customer's time wisely if we don't have a plan, because if you and I sit down to have a conversation, it can go any way it wants to go, and I don't have a plan to keep it on track. I'm not investing my time wisely with my customer, and he's not investing his time wisely with me.

Janet

I think you should always tell your customer how long your presentation is going to take—this presentation is going to take thirty minutes or an hour—and you keep within the frame limits. If the prospect chooses to keep you longer with questions and so on, that's usually a good sign, but I'm going to be careful of his time. When I say thirty minutes, it should be close to thirty minutes, not an hour. I'll lose him that last thirty minutes if I haven't prepared him for the amount of time that I'm going to take from him.

Zig

This is a little dangerous, but it really emphasizes the point. I've heard of one salesman who always takes his watch off and hands it to the prospect. He wears a Rolex, so that's a significant gesture on his part. He says, "If I am here longer than ten minutes, without you specifically inviting me to stay, the watch is yours."

Now you better believe he sells on a plan. By the end of the ten minutes, he instantly has a backup watch so he doesn't overstay his visit, but by the end of about nine minutes, he says, "Well, my time's almost up. The only way I'll stay is by invitation to finish what I have to say." By then, he's strong in the interest stage of his presentation. His point's been well made. The person knows he is a very aware of the importance and value of time, and he's found it to be very effective.

Janet

You make your customer feel very uncomfortable when you're not well-prepared and planned. I've been in front of salespeople, and I'm almost fidgety because they seem not to know where they are in the presentation; they're lost, they're fumbling, they're not sure of themselves. In my mind, this creates the thought, "I'm not sure about buying from you either." So most likely they're going to lose the sale with me, or I would lose the sale if I'm not well-planned in that presentation.

Phil

Doesn't it also say in the mind of many prospects, "That product probably is not that good. That company is probably not that good," because psychologically that's what's being portrayed to them?

On the other hand, if we walk in with a planned, organized presentation, it gives the impression to the prospect—as it should—that I'm dealing with a solid company, a well-prepared salesperson who probably has an outstanding product. That's again one of the benefits of having a well-organized presentation. It makes me be the real professional that I want to be.

Bryan

There has to be some flexibility within that organized presentation. If you're out there making your call, whether it be a referral or whether it be a qualified prospect, you have to gather some needs. Oftentimes, you can't control that, and that's what Jill was mentioning earlier, controlling your time and that person's time.

You have to ask the questions that will get you back on task, as opposed to talking about football games or sporting events or the latest thing happening in local politics. To do that, you really have to be aware of the time, asking and structuring your questions so that you can accomplish the need development, get the needs out, and the buying criteria, as well as keeping on task. That's difficult to do. The better prepared you are, the easier it is to do it.

Jill

Bryan, are you saying you need to have a memorized script?

Bryan

No, I didn't say that. I'm saying you have to be prepared if you have some questions that you need to ask.

Jill

How far should your preparedness go?

Bryan

It's to your comfort level to make the sale.

Janet

I think Bryan's also saying when you are well prepared, it gives you the ability to listen to your customer. Many times, you'll miss something your customer has said because you're not well prepared and you're not listening. You're not able to listen if you're not well prepared in your presentation.

Phil

As for Bryan's point that it enables you to go in and out: if I have a planned, organized, and well-memorized presentation, then I can move right down the track. If the prospect takes me off the track with an objection or a question, that's all right. I can detour, but I can come right back on the track to where I need to be. If I detour again, I come right back on the track to where I need to be. It keeps me moving toward the goal of closing the sale.

Bryan

You've often run into people, who, when you start on your presentation, say, "Time out. Bottom line, what are you selling? What do you do? Let's get rid of all this stuff and get to the point." The hard drivers out there do that, so you have to know your presentation well.

You have to know your visual aids well enough to turn to the part that they're interested in and where they'll say, "Now you're talking my language. Now I'm listening to you." As opposed to other things that you may use that they may think are superfluous and not important. You have to know it well enough to go right into it.

Zig

Psychologists talk a lot about the right brain and the left brain. If we're thoroughly prepared and know every facet of the presentation, then we are utilizing that left brain of ours to its maximum, and that leaves our right brain free to be creative. We have confidence because of our knowledge, expertise, skill, background, memorization, and planning, and then our creative right brain can go absolutely free.

That's what I like about what you all are saying about creative genius, that creative mind. Somebody once said that it was better to copy genius than to create mediocrity. The people who prepared the presentations have had a lot of experience. They might not have been geniuses per se, but they were production geniuses inasmuch as what they have prepared is obviously getting results or it would not be in the training program. So learn what has already proven to be successful. That frees your own creative mind to be more productive in the future.

Janet

Phil, you have some people out on the road that sell, and they make presentations constantly. How do you get them to learn the presentation? Do they write it out word for word? Do they learn it by idea, by thought?

Phil

Janet, we start out memorizing it word for word because that gets it totally ingrained into our consciousness. Then we begin to put our own personalities in it, so that from that point on, all we need is an outline of a word or a phrase. So I'm adapting it to my personality, but initially, we do memorize it word for word.

Janet

So no one presentation is alike. If I were to see any of your salespeople, would each presentation be different?

Phil

It would be slightly different, because each personality would be different, but having that presentation structured in front of them enables them to be reflexive, to listen to the prospect. And as Zig just said, at that point the creative right brain goes to work to develop solutions and sell products.

Jill

Not only do you need to adapt it to make it comfortable for you, but I think you also need to adapt it for your customer. If you've qualified this customer, then you already know what his needs are, what his hot buttons and his objections are going to be. You need to plan that into your presentation, so that when you're talking to that customer, it's not like a form letter, it's like a personal presentation.

Bryan

I find out the buying criteria. If the prospect wants speed, ease, quality, and low cost, I don't want to talk about the other benefits; everything I want to show that prospect during that call is going to be speed, ease, quality, and low cost. We don't want to show something that he's not interested in, and that's the flexibility. That's the left brain and right brain, understanding the procedure and understanding the response from the prospect.

Now that we have that, let's say we're in front of the customer. Now what do we do? Where do we go from there? What are some aids we would use?

Janet

I feel that in my presentations I need visuals. I used visuals all the time in presenting communication systems. I would draw it out for them. If I was planning a communication system, I would show them their entire bank facility, where everything was located, where it was going to go. It was very easy for them to visually see what I was selling.

It's hard to sell wire when you can't see wire. It's hard to sell phones when you can't see phones. So any visual aid that I could have in my hands to show them—and I had large visual aids, depending on the size of the room—I think is very important.

Be sure you plan for your audience. If I have a large audience, can everybody see my visuals? If I have one or two people in the room, what do my visuals need to look like? Is it something in front of them that they pick up, or is it something that I show them?

Jill

Visuals create ownership. If you show me where my communication system is going to go in my floor plan of my office, then it becomes *my* communication system. Another thing you can do, depending on your product, is have them hold it, touch it, feel it, and then take it away: "Thank you, I can take that now." That fear of loss—that's another way you can use your visuals.

Bryan

The best visual in the world is your product, whether it be a phone or a model or whatever. If you can show it, either actually or through literature or brochures, that creates the excitement, the ownership: I can visualize it now. I understand what you're talking about. I see where it fits in the office. I see where it fits in my home, how I could use it, what colors it comes in.

It's amazing what we do. We expect our companies to provide us with support material, literature, fancy brochures, and yet how often do we use them?

At the IBM national training center, there was always a standard routine that we did with the reps coming back after six months on quota. They'd been through months of training at the office. They would come to our training center for a month and then go out and sell. After six months on quota, they'd come back for a two-week course on advanced selling skills.

We would ask them, "Let's see your sales aids. Let's see your manual."

They'd say, "I left it home. I don't have one."

We'd say, "Wait, wait. Why don't you have one?"

"I'm 140 percent of quota; why do I need one?" That was a fair question.

Our question then was, "Wait a minute. You're telling me that you're 140 percent of quota?"

"Yes."

"Are you telling me you'd be less than 140 percent of quota by using this stuff?"

So we really feel that the company should give us the brochures, yet sometimes we don't use them, and that's what we need to do. We have brochures that a lot of money has been spent on. Why don't we use those to bring the customer into the call and make that presentation more effective?

Phil

One skill that I learned many years ago is to pull the visual aid out, put it into the hands of the prospect, get your pencil out, and then point as you're making your presentation. It's incredible: the eyes follow the pen to the content of the brochure. As Zig has taught us many times, we learn a whole lot more when we can see, hear, and do. So the prospect is not only hearing you make the presentation, but they're seeing and reading at the same time, and their eyes are glued to it.

Bryan

I've seen a guy take it one step further. One time a fellow came into my office in San Francisco with his brochures, and he was selling training. Not only did he let me hold, feel, touch, and smell the brochure, he had underlined in yellow highlighter where he wanted my eyes to be drawn to.

Sure enough, that was his presentation. My eye was drawn to this portion, this portion, and this portion—one, two, and three. I remember that it was almost as if I was preparing the call three days in advance with him saying, "Now Flanagan's going to look at point number one first, and then you talk about it. Then, you're going to look at point number two, and you talk about it." He used that technique that you just said, Phil, but he prepared it with underlining. Great technique.

Jill

When you're using aids, there's something that's real basic, and yet I've seen so many salesmen show me their product, and it's kind of beat-up and dirty, because it's the same one they use all the time. Things aren't all together and organized, and that's something that immediately turns me off. That's a basic thing, something we can't forget. If I'm going to show him my product, it has to be great-looking. It has to have no dents in it, nothing like that.

Phil

That takes us back to what we were saying earlier about presenting a professional presentation to a company. On several occasions, we've gone in to make a presentation, and I've reached through to pull out an agreement, and I have found out that it is dog-eared. I put it back and go to the case and get a fresh-looking agreement, because that implies an image of professionalism. On the other hand, it can imply an image that I don't care if I'm going to pull out a dirty piece of literature or something that's not well taken care of.

Bryan

Plus, you leave that with them as you sign that contract. As they press hard, three copies, third copy is theirs. They take that third copy, and that's what they're going to show whomever they need to justify it with, their spouse or whomever. If it looks crumpled or dirty, that doesn't bring up the best image of you or your product to that person.

Zig

I think it goes a lot further than that, actually. If you show them a dog-eared agreement, that would be implying that you've been carrying that thing around too long since you got the last sale. They don't want to do any business with you. Man, I'd have it brand-new and fresh and crisp for sure.

Phil

One of the most effective visuals I've seen is testimonial letters. I'm reminded of the story, Zig, of the salesperson that you worked with who used to roll out an adding machine tape, I believe it was, with the names of all of the people who had become involved in that product.

Zig

The fellow's name was Ralph Beaver. He lived in Greensboro, North Carolina, and he was one of my first characters in the world of selling. He was a showman extraordinaire. He had written down all the names and addresses of all of the customers he had ever sold, and he'd been in the business twenty-five years.

When he would put on a demonstration, he would say, "Now here's some of our customers," and he would unroll it. He would just throw it out, and it would unroll, and he would say, "You might want to see if some of your friends are on the list." He said it used to really tickle him to see them get down on their hands and knees.

That's real showmanship. It is getting the prospect involved. It did arouse interest. It made a very effective part of the presentation.

Phil

As I recall, he also used it as a close with something like, "Would you like for me to go ahead and add your name to this list that we already have?"

Zig

Yes, he sure did. At the very end of it, he'd always use that one. He would say, "As you can see, I've added some blank space down here at the bottom, and we can include your name on this so you can join all of the others." He kind of made a joke out of it, yet it was so impressive to see all of the other people. It was a very effective closing too.

Phil

Let's talk about testimonials for a moment, if we may. We've just established that testimonials are powerful, but how do we get them? Sometimes it seems difficult for us to be able to get testimonial letters, and some salespeople hesitate to use them. How do we go about getting testimonials and then making them useful?

Bryan

It's as easy as asking. It could be as hard as writing it yourself and letting them type it on their letterhead, but the first step is, you must ask.

Janet

I like to get testimonials right after I've been to an account. Let's say they're excited, they're enthusiastic. I'll ask them, "I look forward to hearing from you, and if you would write me a letter about what we did today and how you felt about it and what you liked about it, just drop me a line." Usually it's on their business letterhead, and I rarely fail to get one, whether it's good or bad. If it's bad, I won't use it, but if it's good, I'll use it.

But I'd always ask soon after you've delivered a product or when someone's excited with you. They're more apt to give it to you, rather than calling them a year later, and saying, "By the way, would you mind writing me a letter about how you liked your product?" It almost sounds like, "I really need that, so could you send it on?"

Jill

Not only do you want to ask them right then, but also write a follow-up letter: "I enjoyed coming out there. I enjoyed whatever it was." At the end: "Look forward to hearing the results." That's just another reminder, "Oh yes, I haven't done that yet."

Zig

The testimonial will be lots better too when the prospect first starts using the product. Not that they enjoy it any less later on, but by then they've grown accustomed to it. With all that initial excitement and enthusiasm—that's the best time to get that testimonial letter.

Bryan

That's also when the people that are using the equipment may be giving the one-liners about why they like it. This person said, "It's the most convenient thing we've ever used. Increased my productivity." You wouldn't get those earlier, obviously, or later on, when they've gotten accustomed to it and sort of take it for granted.

Phil

Then we put them in our sales presentation book, and as you said, Bryan, we highlight those areas that we want to make sure that our prospects see. Then we can just turn page after page for the prospect.

Bryan

The benefit there is that if we have that book with those testimonials, and somebody wants speed, ease, quality, we don't tell them about all this. We go right to the speed, ease, quality page: "This person also wanted the productivity that this product features.

Read about what he says right here." That way you can flip right through it and hone in on that person's specific criteria.

Janet

Or industry. That's another big one. Who else in my industry—? Many times, as a part of selling, or even closing, if I have a testimonial letter, I say, "By the way, I'd like for you to call Mr. Joe Jones at ABC Company. He's in the same industry you are, and I know you'd have a wonderful conversation with him. See what he thinks about us, because I have that testimonial letter here, and when you call him, I know the kind of feedback you're going to get." So many times it works in that direction also.

Phil

Another way I've seen testimonial letters work is when I'm sitting down planning the presentation. I think ahead of the needs of the prospect and the objections they're going to raise, and I can say, "Oh, I have two or three testimonial letters that speak to that objection." So when I deal with the objection, I'm able to go right to the testimonial letter and talk about this company, which had that same concern. They used the product, and this is what they've said about it.

Janet

I've also tried using an evaluation form. I'll come up with three or four basic questions that my customer has to verbally fill out and ask him if he would answer them in letter form and send it back to me. This is also a form of getting a testimonial letter, but it's an evaluation form for me also.

Zig

What we're doing here is getting our prospects involved in our business, and that is very important if we expect to be successful in that business.

Phil

Zig, in so many years in the cookware business, you used aids and got prospects involved in using the equipment and demonstrating and cooking the meals yourself. That is the epitome of the use of the visual aid and getting your prospect involved with the product at the time of making a sale.

Zig

Absolutely. When I put on a demonstration, I finally learned to utilize the people who where there and let them help. I'd let them put on the food. I'd let them turn the roast. I would let them make the tea. I would let them cook the carrots.

I would let them do those things, and the more involved they got, the more they saw how easy it was. It wasn't some magic that I had. The sales percentage increased rather substantially as a result of it.

There's always that unspoken fear that the prospect is not going to be able to use whatever it is that you're selling. So when you put them behind the wheel, when you let them operate that machine, when you let them use this piece of equipment, then they know they can do it, because they've already done it.

Bryan

We teach that in effective business presentations: one of the vital skills is audience involvement. In this case, it may be prospect involvement, that shared ownership which Jill mentioned earlier, the fact that, "Yes, I have touched it. It is not as bad as I thought it would be. It isn't that heavy. It's nice. It feels good." With all the things we can do to get them involved to share that ownership, we can act on the as-if principle, as if they were owning it right now. That's key.

Janet

I think in presentation skills, eye contact is vital. I say talk *to* me, not *at* me. Many times how do we use those skills in a presentation? Are we actually talking to our customer so that he becomes a part of it, or are we just simply talking at him?

Jill

Or, talk to me and not to the visual aids.

Zig

That's one reason why a smart salesperson, unless they have a serious eye problem, will never wear dark glasses. There's a certain element of distrust if you can't see the whites of their eyes.

In the world of selling, as you know, there's the statement "I didn't trust that fellow. He never would look me in the eye." Well, I'm here to tell you the biggest and most effective con artists I've ever known in my life could look you dead center with those dark browns or those baby blues, and charm the ears off of a billy goat and lie to you like you can't believe it, but the bottom line is this: if the salesperson will not look the prospect in the eye, the prospect simply does not trust them.

They don't always buy if you *do* look them in the eye, but they're far more likely not to buy if you don't, so make that a point. Unless you have an eye problem, make certain that you have glasses that are clear when you're talking with your prospects.

Janet

I think we also make the point about being excited about your presentations, whether it's the beginning of the day or the end of the day, because that presentation is your involvement with the customer. Be enthused about it. Be excited. Make it a fun experience for the customer, because if you do, they'll remember you when you walk out, compared to someone else who didn't.

Jill

When my presentation is planned, I can allow myself to have that enthusiasm and excitement, because I'm not thinking so hard about what I am going to say next. That's there, so I can be excited about my prospect or my product and have that enthusiasm to show that. Planning has helped me in having that excitement fresh at the end of the day as well as the start of the day.

Phil

It always take me back to something I heard Zig say many years ago: enthusiasm and sincerity will sell far more product than any tool or any technique. That excitement does sell, because it's the transference of feeling.

Zig

The first thing, of course, in a planned presentation is you have to get the *favorable* attention of your prospect. It's easy to get attention, but it must be *favorable* attention. You have to do something to arouse their favorable interest in what you're doing.

What are some of the benefits you can bring out almost immediately? As salespeople, we need to start off with the very strongest point or feature about whatever it is that we're selling. We need to terminate our presentation with the *next* to strongest feature or benefit that our product or service has to offer.

The reason is simply this: a lot of times, they will not be listening to everything you say. Sorry about that, salesperson, but their minds will have a tendency on occasion to drift. When you open up, you generally have their attention, and as you start to wind up—"and the last point I really want to make"—I guarantee you the antennae goes up, and they're listening. They might not always get what you say in between, but they will have gotten the two strongest points that you have.

The conviction step is actually the third step in a presentation. This is reinforced and enhanced tremendously by what we've been talking about here with a lot of good, valid testimonials and vivid demonstrations, which they were participating in. They're convincing themselves when they participate. Testimonials from other people who have no ax to grind but are simply sold on the product will many times be more convincing than the salesperson will be.

Then you have to arouse the desire of that individual to own what you're selling. How do you do that? Basically, desire is aroused by letting that individual understand, not what the product is, but what the benefits are. They do not buy what the product is; they buy what the product does.

Probably the oldest example or illustration of that is this. Last year, in excess of a half million quarter-inch drills were sold. Yet nobody wanted a quarter-inch drill. What they wanted was a quarter-inch hole.

I'm not interested in four tires, a steering wheel, or an automobile body. I am interested in smooth, safe, efficient, comfortable transportation. A lady doesn't want a bunch of paint in a little round tube or a bunch of liquid in a bottle, but she does want a far more attractive appearance and a very pleasant odor that will almost require an insurance policy when she wears it.

Finally, of course, we have to close the sale. I have had some people say, "If you do everything else, the close is automatic." Don't you believe it. A lot of people hesitate to make decisions. We have to prod gently, and we have to use our techniques and procedures in helping them to arrive at the decision which is going to be in their best interest.

Later on we'll give any number of closes, but we absolutely must develop the conviction and the closes if we're going to be effective in closing.

Finally, here's a story about a man who came home one evening, and his little seven-year-old son was doing a little work out in the backyard. He was building a fort. I guess all kids like to do that. There was one heavy post the youngster was trying to move. That youngster was struggling and straining. He was trying so hard to lift it.

His daddy watched him a couple of minutes, and he said, "Son, use all your strength."

The little boy looked at him. He said, "Daddy, you've been watching me. You know I'm trying. I *am* using all my strength."

The daddy said, "No, son, you're not using all your strength."

"Yes, I am, Daddy. I tried hard."

"Son, you didn't ask me to help you. You didn't use *my* strength."

As salespeople, we need to use all the strength available. That strength is the knowledge, the background, the experience, the expertise, and the support materials, which our company can provide us, and which we can learn through books, recordings, and seminars.

We do not have time to have all of the experiences. We must use the successful experience of others. The exciting thing is, when you're using other people's experience, you really are only using successful experience. When you try to have it all yourself, then you have to include in there part of the success and part of the failure.

If you're going to sell right to the right people, use the strength that is available. It is amazing how much there is there. When you do that, you'll be far more successful, and you'll be using one of the most important aspects of *The Secrets of Successful Selling.*

7

CHAPTER

Buyers Must See What You Say

Zig

Somebody once said that one picture was worth a thousand words. Well, the individual who said that obviously never really read the Declaration of Independence. They've never read Lincoln's Gettysburg Address. They've never really read the Twenty-Third Psalm. All of those were words; they were just words. Think of the impact they've had on the lives of so many millions of people.

Charles Osgood expressed it this way: "Compared to the spoken word, the picture is a pitiful thing indeed." Now that's pretty strong, but that's one reason I am always so disturbed when I hear someone, especially a salesperson, using, profane, barnyard language. I've never yet heard of that kind of talk creating a sale, but boy, I've heard of lots of cases where it cost the sale.

You see, words do paint pictures, and a picture needs to be the right one. In times gone past, I've been called a merchant, and to be honest, I'm kind of proud of that designation. But let me suggest that there is a danger for the professional salesperson in talking and in the use of questions and listening.

That's a very important distinction we need to make. Interactive selling skills will help you find the right balance between painting vivid word pictures, asking those all-important questions, and listening to understand the prospect's real objection. After you finish this, I believe you will actually look forward to your prospect's objections. So let's get going right now.

From time to time, I have people ask me, "How do you want me to introduce you for the program? Do you want me to introduce you as a speaker?" I always say, "No. Please tell them I am a teacher."

You see, speakers inform people. They often inspire them. They often entertain them, but teachers give them something which they can take home and use that day, that week, that month, that year. It will have a big and different impact in their lives.

Some words are negative, and some words are positive. My friend, sales trainer Tom Norman, has put together a list of words. Some are negative, some are positive. First of all, let's look at some of those positive words.

The first positive word, of course, is the prospect's name. We all agree that's a very positive word.

Understand is a positive word. *Proven, healthy, easy, guaranteed, money, safety, save, new, love, discovery, right, results, truth, comfort, proud, profit*—oh, we like that one, don't we, businesspeople?—*deserve, happy, trust, value, fun, vital*. Yale University adds a few to that list. *You* is a positive word, *security, advantage, positive, benefits*, and of course, two of the most beautiful words of all, *faith* and *hope*.

There are some negative words, and they're the ones you want to avoid as much as is humanly possible. *Deal*. I can't imagine a professional salesperson using the word *deal*. *Cost, pay, contract, sign, try, worry, loss, lose, hurt, buy, death, bad, sell, sold, price, decision, hard, difficult, obligation, liable, fail, liability, failure*. One of my least favorite of all words in the sales vernacular is *pitch*. I, again, cannot imagine a professional using that word. Of course, profanity is an absolute no-no. The worst of all is God's name taken in vain.

It's important to use the right words, the positive motivating ones, and eliminate the negative, demotivating ones. We need to build our presentation around the positive records so that you can be certain not to use "You know what I mean?" A lot of times the salesman gets to talking, and you know everything he says after you've been listening to him a minute or two: "You know what I'm saying when I'm talking about this, don't you?"

Have you ever been around somebody who had you climbing the wall in about nine seconds flat when they keep saying the same thing over and over? "Understand what I'm saying? Understand what I'm saying? I mean, do you understand what I'm saying? You know what I mean? You know what I mean? You know what I mean?" You go bananas.

Then occasionally I've been around somebody who has just been told you're supposed to use the prospect's name all the time, so what do they do? They use the name. "Well, Mr. Jones, here's the thing, Mr. Jones. Mr. Jones, if you'll follow this, Mr. Jones. Mr. Jones, what you'll find, Mr. Jones, Mr. Jones, is this, Mr. Jones," and in a couple of minutes, again it's driving you out of your gourd.

That's the reason we need to be aware of those words. It's the reason we need to regularly record our presentations and listen back to hear what we're saying. Words can make a dramatic difference. I became aware of this several years ago when I was in Indianapolis, Indiana, having a meal there at the Hyatt Hotel.

They brought that menu out, and when I looked at it, I thought to myself, "Oh, brother, we have a salesperson with a verbal paintbrush who really knows how to use words." I read it, and listen to this: "Spanish Supreme, a tumultuous arrangement of fresh spinach leaves mingled with enoki mushrooms." Do you know what enoki mushrooms are? Tell me the truth. Don't they sound good? "Crisp chips of bacon and ripe tomato with our superb, hot bacon dressing."

Listen to this one. "For protein lovers, Mr. Chopped Sirloin conducts an orchestra of fresh vegetables, fruits, and eggs to an audience of shredded lettuce, with an accompaniment of frozen yogurt and cottage cheese." Can you imagine a better use of words?

The professional takes that verbal paintbrush and paints his prospect right into the picture, giving them the satisfaction and gratification of visualizing the use and enjoyment of what they are selling—one of the most fascinating little incidents of life. A blurb is all it really is, and yet it says so much.

Several years ago, *The New York Times* ran a story about a Mr. and Mrs. Lowe, a New Jersey couple who were having to sell their home. The real-estate people ran an ad, and the ad was beautifully written. It was factual, and it read like this. "Cozy, six-room home. Ranch-style with fireplace. Garage. Tile baths, all hot water heat. Convenient to Rutgers campus, stadium, and golf courses, and a primary school."

Those are facts, but we as professional salespeople need to clearly understand that people do not buy facts. They don't even buy benefits for that matter, unless they can see those benefits translated into their own personal use.

That ad ran for three months, and that house still had not sold. Mrs. Lowe decided to take matters into her own hands. Headlines were, "We'll miss our home. We've been happy in it, but two bedrooms are not enough for us, so we must move. If you like to be cozy by a fire while you admire autumn woods through wide windows, protected from the street, a shady yard in the summer, a clear view of winter sunsets, and quiet enough to hear frogs in the spring but prefer city utilities and conveniences, you might like to buy our home. We hope so. We don't want it to be empty and alone at Christmas." The next day she had six calls and sold the house to one of the callers.

Let's look back at that ad and explore the pictures there. First of all, "we'll miss our home." When you think about that picture, you get a feeling of sadness. Here this couple is: they love their home.

"We've been happy in it." You see the second picture there, but "two bedrooms"—you see, that's not negative about the house. All it says is it's not big enough for us, and it also is factual. It's telling them how much room there is. "Two bedrooms is not enough for us. So we must move."

"If you like to be cozy by a fire"—and who doesn't, really?—"while you admire autumn woods through wide windows." Can't you see that picture? Looking out of those wide windows in the autumn and seeing all of the color, but "protected from the street." You see, it's safe. It's secluded. It gives you and your family privacy. "A shady yard in the summer, cool, and enjoyable. A clear view of winter sunsets." Now that's romance, and "quiet enough to hear frogs in the spring." I don't know what you think about frogs, but all of a sudden, I thought they were pretty nice.

"If you prefer city utilities and conveniences, you might like to buy our home. We hope so. We don't want it to be empty and alone at Christmas." You almost felt sorry for the house, didn't you? I mean, you don't want that house to be alone like that.

Word pictures sell because they appeal to the heart, and people buy with the heart. Everybody is a salesperson, as you've heard me say, and everybody sells. So selling words are extremely important.

One of the greatest salespeople I have ever met is a dentist. His name is Tom McDougall. I'll never forget when I went to see Tom for the first time professionally. I'd been hearing about him. Members of our staff had been over to him, and so I went over to see Tom. I had to have some teeth capped, and I was really impressed with several things.

First of all, three people worked on me before I ever got to Dr. McDougall, and each one of the three smilingly said exactly the same thing. "Mr. Ziglar, Dr. McDougall suggests that you only floss those teeth you want to keep." Now that really said something to me. It says here's a man who is interested in preventive dentistry. He wants me to keep my teeth. I really got a charge out of that.

Dentist consultant Gladys Cook compiled the words that they used at Dr. McDougall's office and other offices, of course. Over there they talk about *restoration*, not *filling*. People don't want to have their teeth filled. They talk about a *change in schedule*. They never use the word *cancellation*. I was in their *reception room*, not their waiting room.

When I got ready to go, they wanted to know how I was going to *take care of*, not pay for the services. They called to *confirm the appointment*, not to remind me. They wanted me to *empty my mouth*, not spit. They *prepared* my teeth. They didn't grind on them. I *received an injection*, not a needle or a shot. I did feel a little *pressure*, but not pain.

Any professional has a moral obligation to sell his services, if they're good. For example, I have a close friend who went to another dentist at about the same time. This friend had nine teeth he needed to have capped. He also was fully covered with insurance, but when he looked at the bill for nine teeth, he just saw, "That's so much money, I'm not going to ask that insurance company to pay that."

So he asked the dentist, "Do I really need to get all nine of them done right now?" The dentist said, "No. Five of them you need to do right now, but the other four can wait." Now he prepared those five teeth. He never said another word, didn't even ask him about insurance, didn't ask when he was going to do it, and though my friend has been back to that dentist two or three times since then, he still has not completed the job with the other four.

I say that dentist did not perform the services that he should have performed as a professional. There are several factors involved. First of all, when my friend goes back, the chances are they're not going to be able to cosmetically match the new caps with the old ones. They can get close, but they won't be cosmetically as attractive.

Number two, there's going to be another investment of several hours, and there will be some additional pain involved. Number three, there will be some additional expense involved, and number four, and probably the most serious of all, is the fact that my friend stands a chance of losing one of those teeth. I believe the professional needs to look it at from the prospect's best interest.

Everybody sells. I never will forget when the pastor of our church sent a couple of men out to see me to ask if I would teach the Sunday School class in the auditorium. Well, that's quite a responsibility, and it was something I was not certain I was qualified to handle because that's a rather conservative church. Of course, I'm conservative, but it was a very big class, and I didn't know if I was ready to tackle it.

"I'm flattered that you've asked," I said. "I really do not know. I will certainly carefully consider it, and then I will pray about what I should do."

The next day I got a letter from the pastor saying, "Thank you for agreeing to teach this class." Now you're talking about the assumptive attitude. All of us are in the world of selling.

When my oldest daughter was three years old, we were up in Knoxville, Tennessee. We had our brand-new baby there at home, and when the baby was about four or five days old, not long after the wife had brought her home, I was caught out on the mountainside and spent the night on the road. Fortunately, I was trapped next to a Greyhound bus, and I had a chance to go in and enjoy some comfortable heat there.

I came home reasonably comfortable, but when I walked in, it was snowing again, and it was cold, and I was absolutely exhausted. I walked in and immediately started pulling my coat off. My wife said, "Honey. Wait a minute, don't take your stuff off yet. We have to go back to the store and get something for the baby." I said, "Oh, OK."

So I started putting the clothing back on, a big topcoat and all, and my three-year-old daughter, Suzie, came up to me and said, "Daddy, I want to go." I said, "Oh, Suzie, the weather's too bad. I'll be back in just a few minutes." But, she said, "Daddy, I'll be so lonely." I said, "Oh, Suzie, you're not going to be lonely. Your mother is here. The maid's here. Your little sister is here."

She looked at me, and she said, "Yes, Daddy, but I'll be lonely for you." Everything is selling. I don't think I need to tell you that she went with me to that grocery store to get whatever it was we had to get.

As a salesperson, you should capitalize on the natural things that you have, the obvious things which are yours to work with. If you're a lady, for example, have you ever shown up all of a sudden in a beautiful dress that your husband did not know you had gotten, and he backs away, looks at it, and says, "Ooh" or "Ahh"?

Why is it that salesladies sometimes set aside those very special garments for their special customers,? "Oh, Mrs. Jones, this is our ooh dress. When you show up with this at home, your husband is going to take one look and say *ooh*." If that's not picture selling, I don't know what is.

I'm a golf enthusiast. I love to hit golf balls. We've done some work with the PING Manufacturing Company. Actually, they have the set of clubs that I'm using. I think they're fantastic. If I were selling golf clubs, you know the line I would use from time to time for these avid golfers. I'd say to them, "Now this is our set of ooh and ahh clubs, because when you step up to that tee and bust that ball right down the middle, your friends are going to say ooh or ahh."

I've been amazed at the number of times I have overheard conversations between ladies. One of them will say, "You know, my husband bought me a dress. I wear a size 13, and he came home with an 8. I cannot believe that he did such a dumb thing." Or "he showed up with green, and he knows I look terrible in green."

I've been married now for well over forty years. I've bought my wife dozens and dozens of gifts, and I'm delighted to be able to say I have never made a mistake, not even once. I always get the right size, I always get the right color, I always get exactly what she was dreaming and hoping that I was going to get.

I'll be the very first to admit that frequently I never see it again, because she has taken it down and gotten something that did fit and that she did want, but what is she doing? She is giving me all the encouragement I possibly could use.

That's selling. That's selling of the highest order, where you paint the pictures, where you use the words, where you paint that prospect into the picture, where you give hope and encouragement.

I never will forget that Friday evening when the redhead met me out at the airport. I'd been gone all week, and she met me there. She was dressed in one of those ooh and ahh dresses. Had on some of that good, sweet-smelling stuff. While we were waiting for my bag to come down, she snuggled up real close, slipped her hand into mine; she's powerful friendly anyhow.

She looked up at me and said, "Honey, you know, I was just thinking. You've been gone all week. I know you've been in five different cities. You have to be tired having done all these seminars. If you would like, on the way home, we'll stop by the store, and we'll pick up some fish, some seafood, or maybe a nice steak, and when we get home—Tom's spending the night down the street—and it'll just be the two of us.

"It won't take me long to prepare us a really nice dinner, and the two of us will sit there and just really enjoy the meal. I know you don't want to get involved in washing a whole bunch of dirty, greasy pots and pans and dishes and cleaning up. It shouldn't take me more than an hour, hour and a half, two hours at the most."

But, she said, "The thought occurred to me that you would probably be far more comfortable if I were free to devote the entire evening just paying attention to you. I could do that, of course, at a really nice restaurant."

Everything is selling. Everything is persuasion, and so long as you understand the concepts that I'm talking about here, you can have everything in life you want if you will just help enough other people get what they want.

I close with these two thoughts. The professional salesperson doesn't smoke or drink on sales calls. Now I know what you're thinking: "Suppose the other person is smoking." But I'm going to tell you that you're going to miss some sales. I don't know which one or when it will take place, but over a period of time, I'm here to tell you that you will miss some sales because you're smoking on the call.

It takes time to light up. It takes time to take a drag off that cigarette. You have to put the fire out and give it enough time. The day's going to come when you're going to get excited and lay that cigarette down care-lessly, and you're going to end up burning a credenza or a desk or a sofa. You also will offend some people. It simply is not worth it. Do not smoke on sales calls.

A lot of times people say, "You said something about not taking a drink. You mean you don't take a drink with your clients?" Yes, I'm absolutely con-vinced that you make a mistake when you take a drink with a client. What do you do when they offer you one? You say no. You simply say no.

Suppose they insist? In all the years of my career, I have never had as many as ten people absolutely insist, and when they insist, I always just quietly say, "No, I just don't drink." Of the ten, if I'm not mis-taken, at least five of them said, "Man, I wish I didn't." It did not cost me a sale. In a lot of cases, it made me a friend, and I end up getting more business.

I've seen a lot of business lost even after it is gained when somebody cannot handle their booze. In too many cases, the booze eventually ends up han-dling you. Sales come unglued because a person got a little tight, got too familiar with a prospect.

I've had salespeople say to me, "When I take a drink, it relaxes me." If that's what it does to the other person, you're still even. Some people say, "It sharpens me up." If it does that for you, that's what it does for the other person, and you're still even.

But I challenge you as to whether it really does sharpen you up. If you really believe that, let me ask you a question: if you were faced with major surgery, you would want the surgeon to be at his best and sharpest. Are you going to insist that he has a little nip just before he opens you up? I don't think so.

I'm talking about selling more. Overall, over a period of time, I'm convinced beyond any doubt that, yes, you can sell more with no smoking and no drinking.

Finally, the professional is health-conscious. I cannot believe that we, as salespeople, do not take better care of our health. A lot of times people say, "I don't have time." Let me share this with you. When I got involved in an exercise program some fifteen or sixteen years ago, that question was on my mind. When am I going to have time?

I discovered that I have so much to do that I do not have time *not* to take care of my health. At lunch, for example, if it were practical and convenient for you to take a good fifteen or twenty-minute workout, you'd be amazed at how much more productive you would be that afternoon.

There's a physiological, not just psychological, reason for that. When you exercise, you activate the pituitary gland. The pituitary gland floods the system with endorphins over 200 times as powerful as morphine. For the next two to five hours, you are on a natural chemical high. Your energy level is higher. Your creativity is higher.

Remember—the last hour of the day is when you should be at your best and most effective. That's when you can do your best selling. The last prospect you see deserves just as much energy, just as much enthusiasm, just as much professionalism as the first one you saw that morning. And because his or her energy level is beginning to run down a little, if you're in great physical, mental, emotional condition, your chances of having that extra bit of enthusiasm and energy necessary to make the sale will be greatly enhanced.

I'm convinced. No question about it—when you're taking care of yourself, you'll be more effective in the sales process. You bet you. That's one of the most important secrets of successful selling.

8

CHAPTER

Questions are the Answer

Zig

Chances are excellent that you've noticed something that virtually all professionals have in common: every one of them is tastefully and conservatively dressed. The reason is very simple. Countless, and I do mean countless, psychological studies reveal that the appearance of the counselor—and that is what a professional salesperson is—has a direct bearing on whether or not the advice given is going to be followed.

The second thing that professionals, whether they're doctors, lawyers, ministers, accountants, tax consultants, guidance counselors, architects, psychiatrists, or salespeople, have in common is they ask a lot of questions. The reason is fairly obvious. The professional must identify your problem, your need or desire. They have to find out what you want and what you need before they can offer the solution.

They also know that if they ask you the right question, you will often come up with the solution. That way it's your idea, so your chances of enthusiastically following through are dramatically increased. For the professional salesperson, the advantages are obvious, because it bears out the concept that you can have everything in life you want—in this case more sales—if you'll just help another people get what they want—in this case a solution to the problem.

Incidentally, the professional also directs the interview so that the prospect or person being counseled asks questions so that he, the expert, can give advice which is relevant to the prospect's needs and concerns. That's really what's it's all about.

In a nutshell, selling isn't just telling, it's asking. I'm obviously not talking about the police interrogator or the prosecuting attorney approach, where they put you on the griddle. I'm talking about the counselor-consultant, the helpful friend approach.

Let me share with you a story out of my own sales background. As I do, I want you to notice the number of questions that go back and forth. I also want to encourage you to notice something that when we reach a particular area of the questioning. This is where the salesperson's self-image is so important.

Because of a fear of rejection, or a fear they're going to offend somebody, or a fear they're going to miss that sale, a lot of people are a little bit weak when they start to nail down some of their points.

In 1962, I was selling in the cookware business. I was in Columbia, South Carolina. I've always believed in nest selling. By that I simply mean I believe in selling in a small area. When I was in the life-insurance business, I used to work in one large building or one very small town. I've always felt that if you get in the car for a long trip with a half-million prospects next door, you ought to put on a chauffeur's hat, because that's really what you're doing. You're just driving around.

Anyhow, the little town of St. Matthews, South Carolina, was at that time about twenty-five miles from my back door in Columbia, South Carolina. I got started in that area, and we put on the group demonstrations at night. In less than six months, I sold over $40,000 worth of cookware in that little, bitty town. In those days, that was a powerful lot of cookware.

I'll never forget one evening when I had a demonstration for seven couples. The next day, as I was making my calls, I sold the first five and knocked on the door for the sixth one. A booming voice came forth, "Come on in, Mr. Ziglar."

I walked in, and there stood this big fellow. He had been there the evening before with his wife. He was about six feet, six or seven inches tall and weighed over 300 pounds, but he was not fat. He was just a big man.

As I walked in, he said, "Glad to see you. Me and you both know I ain't going to buy no $400 set of pots, but it's good to see you." Now let me emphasize that that old boy had eaten food the night before in direct proportion to his size. I had bought that food, I had cooked that food, and I had served that food, so his introduction to our interview wasn't exactly ideal as far as I was concerned.

When he said that, I grinned and said, "No, sir. I did not know it. You might have, but I didn't." He said, "Well, might as well be up front and tell you. I'm glad to talk to you because I understand that's part of the deal so the hostess can get her prize, but I'm not about to buy no $400 set of pots."

I grinned and said, "Mr. Prospect, it looks like you and I have lots in common."

He said, "Oh, how's that?"

"In my particular case," I said, "my wife spends our money, and the neighbors take care of our business, and all I have to do is work. Now I don't know what your situation is as far as your wife is concerned, but I can tell you neighbors are taking care of your business."

"Oh," he said, "how's that?"

He was a very jovial fellow, and I said, "Well, I've been to five places, and in every case, after they had gotten their set of cookware"—I had to slip that one in—I said, "they would all ask me what did Mr. So-and-So do. I said I hadn't seen him yet. They'd say, 'Let me know what he does.' I finally asked one of them, 'Why does everybody want to know what this particular individual does?'"

The old boy laughed. He said, "They probably told you I was the biggest tightwad in the county."

I said, "One of them did say something about the first dollar, but I'm not sure I understood what he meant."

He laughed and said, "Me and you both know you knew exactly what he meant."

"Yes, I guess I did," I said, "but isn't that amazing? You were born and raised right here in this little area."

"Yes, never left five miles from here."

"Isn't that amazing? You were born and raised right here, and nobody here really knows anything about you."

"What are you talking about?"

"I thought you said you were not going to get the cookware."

"I'm not."

"Isn't that amazing? You were raised around these people. None of them know you."

"Explain what you're saying."

"Mr. Prospect, let me ask you a question. Last evening, were you sincere"—don't ever ask anybody if they're telling you the truth; that's an insult—"when you said you knew that your family could save at least a dollar a day cooking in our set of cookware?" We'd made a big to-do about demonstrating the economy.

"Mr. Ziglar," he said, "I'll tell you. As big as my family is, I could save $2 a day. I have four boys, and they're all bigger than I am, and they all eat more than I do, and you know how much I ate last night. I could save $2."

"A dollar a day, then, would be very conservative, wouldn't it?"

"It sure would."

"Then if I cut that dollar half in two—a half a dollar a day—that would be ultraconservative, wouldn't it?"

"Yes, it would."

Notice this. Then I said to him, "Well, if that set of cookware would save you fifty cents a day, that means it costs you fifty cents a day *not* to have it, doesn't it?"

"Well," he said, "I suppose you could say that."

"No, sir. What I say is not important. I'm talking about your money, so what do *you* say?"

"Well, I suppose I could say the same thing."

I said, "No, sir, now we can take that *suppose* out, can't we?"

"You're the most persistent guy I think I've ever seen."

"I'm talking about your money."

"OK, we'll take it out. Yes, I could save fifty cents a day."

"Then," I insisted, "that means it costs you fifty cents a day *not* to have that set of cookware."

He said, "OK, point's made."

"Now, Mr. Prospect, what that really means is this. It means that every two days, your wife will take a dollar out of the family till, and because she does not have this method of preparing the food and saving shrinkage and electricity and all of that, it means that she literally every two days will take a dollar out of the family treasury and tear that $1 bill all to pieces. Every two days she will do that, and it really amounts to the fact that she'll just throw it away.

"Now," I said, "Mr. Prospect, that's not so bad. I mean from what your neighbors tell me, and please understand, I'm smiling when I'm saying this. According to what your neighbors say, $1 is no big deal. They tell me these 1100 acres of good fertile land under cultivation don't belong to you and the bank. They belong to you. This beautiful home does not belong to you and the savings and loan. It belongs to you.

"But, according to your neighbors, you sure do hate to see something happen to one of them dollars. That's not so bad until you realize that on that program, that every forty days, your wife will reach in and pull out a brand-new $20 bill out of the family treasure, and she will take that brand-new $20 bill, and she will tear it all to pieces and just throw it away." I took out a $20 bill and tore it up.

When I tore that money up, cold sweat broke out on his forehead, and I asked him, "Mr. Prospect, what did you think when I tore up that bill?"

He said, "I thought you were crazy."

"Mr. Prospect, whose money was that?"

"I hope it's yours."

"It is," and I said "Yet you hated to see me tear up my money, didn't you?"

"I sure did."

"Mr. Prospect, don't you feel even closer to the money that is your very own?"

"What are you getting at?"

I said, "Mr. Prospect, as I understand it, you've been married nearly twenty-three years."

"Yes, it'll be twenty-three years in August."

"I don't know how to multiply times twenty-three," I said, "but I'm a whiz at multiplying times twenty. From what you have told me today, you believe that you could save fifty cents a day by having our set of cookware, or it'll cost you fifty cents a day not to have it. That's $182.50 a year. I want to switch it back to $180, because I can multiply times $180 real easy. That means, Mr. Prospect, that in twenty years, you have already invested—*paid* is a better word for it, *wasted* maybe—$3600 not to have a set of our cookware. Now you tell me you won't invest $400 to have a set of the cookware.

"Mr. Prospect, that's government thinking if I have ever seen it in my life, but that's not so bad, because maybe you didn't know about this until now. Now you're saying to me, 'Look, Mr. Ziglar, in the next twenty years, I'm going to spend another $3600 in waste for a total of $7200 not to have a set of the cookware, but I'm not going to give you $400 to own a set of the cookware.'"

I said—I'm smiling when I'm saying this—"Now, Mr. Prospect, I hate to threaten anybody, but in your case I'm going to make an exception. I'm going to ruin your reputation in this community if you don't buy a set of my cookware, and the reason is very simple. These people, your friends, they think you are conservative, but me and you both know that any time a man will spend $7200 not to have a set of our cookware and won't give $400 to own a set of the cookware, he is not conservative. He is a wild-eyed liberal for sure."

It got awful quiet for a minute, and he asked something that really impacted my sales career. He said, "Mr. Ziglar, what could I tell my neighbors?" Very significant. You see, people buy for two reasons: for themselves and for other people. They might say it doesn't make any difference what anybody else is doing. Don't you believe it in most cases.

Why would he ask that question, and why must we include some logic and some facts for them to make their decisions on simply so they can tell their friends, relatives, and neighbors why they bought it? You see, this man had told the hostess when she invited him, "I'll come eat the man's food. I'm not going to buy no $400 set of pots." The night of the demonstration, he was late arriving. When he walked in, they got to kidding him. "Hey, partner, I see you've come to buy that $400 set of pots." You know how good friends kid each other.

He said, "I ain't going to buy no $400 set of pots. I've come to eat the man's food."

Now he's asking, "What can I tell my neighbors?" He's painted himself in a corner. Many times, prospects do that. They paint themselves in a corner.

They've told another salesman six months ago, "If I ever buy the machine, I'll get it from you."

They've even forgotten his name, or it might be another case where they're legitimately in the corner. If we can get them out, the sale is a foregone conclusion. I knew the sale was mine if I could get the man out of the corner. "What will I tell my neighbors?"

"I'm going to give you some words to use," I said, "and if you'll do this, not only will your neighbors love you even more, but they will respect you even more. I'm going to go ahead and write this up, and I'm going to mark it *paid in full* because I know you're not going to fool around paying interest since you're a conservative individual," and we both laughed when I said that.

"I'm going to give you the receipt written out across the top, *paid in full*, and I'm going to suggest that you take this and go to see each of your friends, and when you walk in, just wave the slip of paper. They'll recognize it, because they have one the same color. When you walk in, be prepared. They're going to razz you like you've never been razzed before. Just stand there and grin. Let them go ahead and do it.

"When they get through, here's what you need to tell them. You look at them and say, 'Yes, I clearly said I wasn't going to get it, but when I made that statement, all I knew was the price. I had no idea what the benefits were, and when I realized it would be better for my family, that it would save my wife work, and for that matter would save me some money, and when I realized that I could not let my own stubbornness stand in the way of doing something for my family, especially since I had the money, I bit my tongue and went ahead and bought it.'

"Mr. Prospect," I said, "they'll love you more because it takes a big man to admit he made a premature decision. It takes an even bigger one to do something about it."

The old boy sat there for fully a half minute. He slapped his leg. He got up and said, "You're the doggonest fellow I've ever seen in my life," and he headed back to the back bedroom. In the rural South, they keep the checkbook in the back bedroom chest of drawers, third one from the top.

An interesting thing about that particular incident: from that moment on, that old boy became one of my best friends and biggest supporters. As a matter of fact, every time I scheduled a demonstration down there, he would call up and ask the hostess who was coming. The hostess would give him the names, and he'd go down the list. He'd say, "Well, he can sell that one, he can sell that one. He won't have any trouble with that one. Uh-oh, I don't believe he can handle that one. I better go with him on that."

He helped me sell an enormous amount. I believe fervently to this day that had he not seen that demonstration of that money coming apart, he never would have been a customer.

Now I know what you probably are thinking: "Yes, but Ziglar, I don't sell cookware."

That's one of the important things about support material and training sessions that go with this training, and that's the fact that you will be shown more methods of translating it to other situations.

For example, several years ago, we had to buy a new copier. It was long overdue. We figured mathematically that that little old thing we were using, because it was slow and wasted a lot of paper, cost us at least two hours a day. Even at two hours a day, back in those days, it would cost us a minimum of $5 an hour, and it really cost more than that.

So when you start multiplying, if you have $5 an hour, and you're wasting two hours a day, you're talking about $10 a day. You're also talking about $50 a week. Then, if there are fifty weeks in the year, you are talking about $2500 a year that that ineffective, old machine was costing us.

A salesman came along selling a machine that was $10,000. Now I had to ask myself some questions. Do I want to go ahead and invest that $10,000?

Here is the way I mapped it out. If I do invest my $10,000, and assuming that's all I have, then at that moment, I don't have any money left, but I do have the machine, the copier.

A year from now, because it will save me that $2500, I now have $2500 of my money back, and obviously I have the machine. In two years' time, I will have $5000 back, and I'll have the machine. In three years, I will have $7500 back, and obviously I'll have the machine. In four years' time, I will have my full $10,000 back, and I will have that machine.

Let's say I don't invest in the new copier. Obviously my benefit is I've got my $10,000, but I have no machine. Now, a year later, I've only got $7500 because I have invested $2500 in paying that person the $5 an hour. I have, at the end of the first year, no machine. In two years' time, I only have $5000 and no machine. In three years' time, I only have $2500, and I have no machine. In four years' time, I literally don't have any of my money, and I have no machine.

Here's the way I would wind it up. I would say, "Now, Mr. Prospect, here's the decision that you have to make. Look down the road four years. For years from now, if you do invest, you'll have $10,000 and the machine. If you don't invest, you'll have no money and no machine. As a prudent businessman, Mr. Prospect, which do you think is the wiser route to follow?" When you diagram things like that, people can follow you more easily.

If you noticed, we've done a lot of questioning. There are two principles for effective questioning. First of all, questions can be used immediately in the interview to set the stage for sales now and later.

As an example, in a furniture store, let's say that you have a customer walk in and say, "I want to see a coffee table." You know where the coffee tables are, so you head for that area. You take four or five steps, and you turn to the prospect and say, "Let me ask you.

Did you have a specific purpose in mind for this coffee table, or would you like for it to blend in with the rest of your décor so you can get maximum mileage out of your furniture dollars?"

Let's say you're in a clothing store—same principle. A fellow walks in, he wants a jacket or a suit or whatever. You say, "Well, they're over here." You take a few steps, and then you turn to that individual and say, "Let me ask you. Did you want this suit to blend in with the rest of your wardrobe, or did you have a special occasion for it? In short, do you want to maximize your clothing dollars, or does this just meet one special need?"

You zero in on the future sale at the same time you're concentrating on the present sale. Occasionally you'll have a ridiculous request. Somebody might come in and say, "I'd like a four-poster water bed with a canopy." The likelihood of that happening is pretty slim, but you need to find out if they're serious. "I'm curious as to why you want this particular piece of furniture." It might not be a legitimate request. You need to find out early.

In real estate, you're showing a home, and here's what you do. You could say to the prospect, "If this ended, you're in the home with this magnificent living den and kitchen. It's already exciting to see, isn't it?" Or "If this house had nothing but this location, it would merit consideration, wouldn't it?"

If you're demonstrating a computer or a piece of equipment, you can ask, "If this were the only feature this machine had, it would be well worth owning, wouldn't it?" You're asking trial closes. You're asking assumptive questions on occasion too, and a good assumptive close question would be something like this: "When we install the equipment, would you like me to demonstrate the major features again?" It could be something like, "Would you like for me to protect this for you by marking it sold while we check on terms and delivery?" Perfectly natural, normal questions.

"Would you like to have your own bank finance this, or would you prefer that we work out all of the details on it?" There are over 700 questions of a similar nature, which we have written out in "Secrets of Closing the Sale," which is one bit of support material.

Many questions really are thinking questions and help to lead the prospect to the decision. For example, "If you saw that it was to your advantage to own this product, and the terms we work out are satisfactory, would you like to start enjoying the product immediately?" Trial close.

"Do you believe it's wise to invest in solidly constructed equipment, which will give you long, trouble-free operation for the lifetime of the product?" A thinking question. "Would you agree that as a practical matter it is worth what it can do for you and not what you have to pay for it?"

Questions can be used in so many different ways. I vividly remember a number of years ago, I was scheduled to speak in Greenville, South Carolina.

I'd written for a room reservation, but when I pulled into the parking lot there and saw all the traffic, I got a little nervous. When I walked in the front lobby, I knew I was in trouble, because there was a sign that said, "Traveling men, avoid Greenville, South Carolina the week of October 11 through 15. This is Textile Week."

They tell me that during that week, you can't get a room within fifty miles of Greenville, South Carolina. I walked up to the desk. I figured I really had to do something here, so I walked up to the desk, and I said, "My name is Zig Ziglar. Would you mind checking my mail, please?"

The lady was not impressed. "Mr. Ziglar, do you have a reservation?"

I said, "I certainly hope so. I wrote for it long ago."

She said, "How long ago?"

"Oh, it's been nearly three weeks."

"Wait a minute, Mr. Ziglar," she said. "We haven't had an opening here in over a year. We book them from one year to the next."

About that time, a little lady walked out from behind another counter, and she came over. The first clerk was new. She turned to the second one, and she said, "This is Miss Fortune."

I said, "She doesn't look like misfortune to me. She looks like good news all the way."

The lady smiled very pleasantly and said, "Mr. Ziglar, ordinarily I am good news, but unfortunately today for you—"

"Wait a minute, ma'am," I said. "Don't say another thing. I have two questions I need to ask."

She smiled pleasantly and said, "OK, what are they?"

"Question number one, do you consider yourself to be an honest woman?"

"Why, of course, I do."

"All right," I said. "Question number two. If the president of the United States were to walk through that door right there right now, and come up here and say to you, 'I want a room for this evening,' tell me the truth. Would you have a room for him?"

She grinned and said, "Now, Mr. Ziglar, you know perfectly good and well we'd have a room for the president of the United States."

"Ma'am, you're an honest woman," I said. "I'm an honest man. You have my word for it. The president of the United States is not going to come through that door. I'll take his room." I promise you I slept there that evening.

Here is the rest of that story. The group I was speaking for had as its president the manager of that particular motel. He had been unable to get me a reservation in his own motel. He said there were no rooms. I also used it on at least two other occasions.

You can use questions in a lot of ways. Questions are important tie-downs to close the sale. The late Doug Edwards used to do things like this. When somebody would ask the question like, "Does this come in green?" If you just say yes, you still haven't made any progress. Doug taught us to say, "Do you want it if it comes in green?"

When he responds yes to that question, he's bought it. You nail it down with, "We can have it for you in three weeks, or if I put a rush order on it, I can get it in two weeks. Which would you prefer?"

Or someone might ask a realtor, "Do the draperies come with the house?"

"Do you want it if the draperies come with the house?" The professional answers a question with a tie-down. This is beautiful in red, isn't it? The added weight gives much greater comfort, doesn't it? The extra horsepower is a real bonus, isn't it? The additional color gives it an added dimension, doesn't it? This evening view should give you a lot of beautiful memories, shouldn't it?

Isn't, shouldn't, this kind of thing. Each tie-down is emotionally moving the prospect toward a favorable decision. Incidentally, don't use the word *not.* Instead, use *don't, can't, isn't,* that kind of thing.

In alternative-choice closing, we always ask questions. Again, everybody sells. A parent says to the child, "Do you want to cut the grass or wash the windows?" The teacher to the student, "Do you want to settle for a B, or would you prefer to complete the assignment?" The physician to the patient, "Would you like to live longer, or keep on smoking?" The attendant to the car owner, "Would you like for me to rotate the tires and give you an extra 5000 miles or leave them as they are?" The patrolman to the speeder, "Would you like to pay the speeding ticket now, or do you prefer to go to court on the first of August?"

Question. Since all of us sell every day, doesn't it make sense to learn how to do it more effectively? You should commit to memory hundreds of questions. You can use the question technique in all phases of life, but in closing, let's look at two additional qualities of the professional salesperson.

He is appropriately dressed. You can't play the role of success dressed in the costume of failure. This professional salesperson is a time miser. He uses that time.

One of my favorite stories concerns a young man I met when I was in England three years ago. His name is Mike Bagg, and Mike sells sales training. He had driven into this little suburb outside London from the town of Reading. He had thirty minutes before his next appointment.

He walked into this automobile dealership. It was at lunchtime. He asked the lady there where the managing director was, as they say over there. She said, "He's across the street." Mike walked across the street, walked in the office, and he said to the receptionist there, "I would like to see the managing director. Is he in?"

She said, "Yes, he's in the back room."

The managing director had heard Mike when he came in. He walked out, and he started to say something, and Mike said to him, "As the managing director of this company, I'm certain you're always interested in looking for training that will enable you to make more sales and increase your profit margin considerably, aren't you?"

The guy looked at him and said, "Young man, it's lunchtime on Friday afternoon. I am very, very busy. Tell me why in the world would you take this particular time to come calling on me."

Mike said he looked at him very calmly and said, "Do you really want to know?"

"Yes, that's the reason I ask. I really want to know."

Mike said, "I just drove in from Reading. I have thirty minutes before my next appointment. I decided to invest the thirty minutes instead of wasting it. I decided to call on a prospect. Isn't that what you teach your salespeople to do with their time?"

Mike said the guy looked at him almost in awe and said, "Come on in, young man." Mike left there in twenty-five minutes with a substantial order. Yes, the professional uses his time. When you use your time effectively, when you learn to ask questions, when you learn to get people involved in the transaction, you're using some of the most important secrets in successful selling.

Turning Objections into Sales

Zig

It might come as a surprise to you when I say this, but the thing that we salespeople ought to get the most excited about are objections. You see, if there were no objections to begin with, there'd be no need for us as salespeople. People would just go ahead and buy everything, and we would be out of the picture. One of the most important aspects of selling is dealing with those objections.

To begin with, let's understand the basic difference between a question and an objection. A question simply means they're seeking information. How long will it take for delivery? What colors does this come in? A person who raises an objection is looking for encouragement. They are saying, "I have an interest in this, and I want you to give me some encouragement about the way I can end up owning what you are selling." No objections and no interest, I think, go together without any doubt.

Objections are our friends. They clearly say to us as salespeople, "Yes, I am interested in what you are selling." You don't have to answer all objections. That's the first thing that I want to make clear.

For example, this set of clothes I have on. I did not like all of the things about this suit. As a matter of fact, there were two things I didn't like about it, and yet I bought the suit.

What were the two things I didn't like? I wasn't overly excited about the price. I just to have to fess up going in; I wasn't. The second thing I didn't like about it was the fact that I have to wear a belt. I prefer the other kind, but my wife told me it was a nice fit and that the color went well with me. She said, "Honey, I like it." All objections were overcome. I bought the suit.

The third thing about objections is the fact that when you're out in the world of selling, approximately 90 percent of them will be the same. In many cases, what you need is a new presentation or a more conclusive or inclusive presentation, because if the same one keeps coming up, it indicates that you're not doing enough selling in the presentation itself.

Let me say this as point number four. There's a formula which fits in most cases, and you can adapt this formula and follow it in handling objections. However, we need to remember that there are many different kinds of prospects. You have the animal prospect, who's going to bear it in mind, the insomniac prospect, who's going to sleep on it, the musical prospect, who will make a note of it, and the playful prospect, who's just feeling out the market.

I believe we need to clearly understand that all prospects, regardless of what kind they are, have two basic things in common. Number one, they want to be right. Now, salespeople, you can relate to that. You know you want to be right. Number two all of us will relate to also. The prospect wants to be understood.

There are four times and opportunities to handle objections. The first is before they occur, the second time is when they occur, the third time is later on the presentation, and the fourth time is never. Some objections simply should never be given any credibility at all.

By far the most effective place to handle an objection is before it occurs. When the same one keeps coming up, as I said a moment ago, you need to reorganize that presentation.

Many years ago, a man named Harry Lemons, who was the inventor of this particular food-chopping machine, taught me a couple of things that I was really excited about. I used to demonstrate these things at state fairs and on television. I've sold lots of them. When I turned that crank, that food would come tumbling out, and we could make it do tricks. We could make that machine talk cutting those fresh vegetables.

Invariably we encountered two major objections. I'd be right in the middle of the demonstration, and some member of the group there—a lady generally, because they'd be the ones who would end up using it at home—would ask me, "Mr. Ziglar, if I bought that machine, could I use it like you use it?"

I'd always look at her, and I'd smile, and I'd say, "No, ma'am. There's no way that you will ever be able to use this machine like I use it." You might think that's a strange thing for me to say, but I did it for a couple of reasons. Number one, I was telling her the truth. I don't believe there's a housewife in 10,000 who could ever learn to use that machine as I did, and I explained why.

Basically, they have 101 other things to do. They're going to use the machine two or three or four times a week. I was using it several hours every single day. It's not likely that they could do what I could do with it. But how many machines would I have sold if I had stopped it right there? I wanted to sell machines, so here's what I answered with in the presentation.

I'd say, "No, ma'am, you could never use it like I do, because you have so many other things to do, but let me tell you how effectively you can use it. The machine comes with an instruction book, and I can give you this book right now. If you will spend five minutes reading the book, I can give knives," and I'd pick out the three ladies who were closest to me, "I can give the sharpest knives available to these three ladies, and in five minutes' time with this machine, you can cut more food better and faster than all three of these ladies with the knives combined.

"You've never used the machine. They've been using knives all of their lives, but you could cut more with a machine not because you're an expert with the machine but because you have the machine, which does the job, and that's what you really want, isn't it?" I would use that also as a trial close right there.

"As you can see," I'd say, "we have five blades. One blade is on the machine, and there are four other blades, and they'll do an awful lot of things." I would demonstrate one of the blades, and then when I finished demonstrating the first blade, I'd use another trial close. I would have cut about seven or eight foods, and I'd say, "As you can see, we only have used one blade, and we've cut all of this beautiful food. Now ladies, let me ask you. If the machine only had one blade, how many of you already feel that's something that you really want to have in your home? Can I see your hands?"

I would get my best prospects immediately right there. Then, I would demonstrate the rest of the blades.

The second objection that would often come up was people would ask me, "Mr. Ziglar, if I bought that machine, could I cut my hand on it?"

I'd grin, and I'd say, "Yes, ma'am. We don't recommend it, but if that's really what you want to do, it's a very simple procedure. All it takes is coordination. You insert the finger as you turn the crank. Now get it straight. Insert finger, turn crank, and when you do, the red comes out right here. If you don't want to cut your hand, keep it out of the machine."

What is this doing? You're selling on the offense. Your believability is greater if you handle the objections in the body of the presentation. Otherwise you are apparently defending instead of selling on the offense.

Regardless of the kind of prospect, if the objection occurs during the presentation, there are some basics you can follow, especially on the first objection. For example, you might be demonstrating tires, and the prospect might say, "I don't believe these tires are rugged enough for our use." Now what do you do?

Number one, you hear the objection out. Solomon, the wisest man who ever lived, put it this way: "He who answers the matter before he hears it is not wise." Let them get the objection out. Number two, you act pleased that they've brought it up. Objections thrive on opposition, but they die with agreement: "I'm really glad you raised that issue." Don't use the word *objection*, but *raised that issue*. You truly should be glad, because that says, "I'm interested."

Number three, you change the objection to a question: "Your question, as I understand it, is, will these tires hold up under the day-to-day pounding our city streets will give them? Is that what you're asking?" That way you get the customer involved.

Number four, you need to get the commitment that this is the only question: "Mr. Prospect, is this the only question you have which stands between you and an ownership of these tires, or would there be something else?" You obviously wait for the answer.

Number five, you use the question-objection as the reason for going ahead: "Actually, Mr. Prospect," you say, "the question you raise is the reason we do so much business in this city. Fleet test after fleet test firmly established the fact that our superreinforced, steel-belted radials are ideally suited for rugged city street usage. As a matter of fact, that's the very reason that XYZ Company," and then you parade your testimonials, and you close the sale at that point.

If the prospect brings up another objection after you've completed your presentation, handle it in the same manner, but if they bring up yet another objection, you respond with a question: "Mr. Prospect, do you mind if I ask you, is this the only question which stands between you and a favorable decision concerning our product, or would there be something else?"

If that's the only other question, you answer it, you assume the sale, and you attempt to close, but if the prospect says, "Well, I'm also concerned about—" and they start bringing other things out, then you take your talking pad, and whatever the objection might be, you write it down. It might be price, it might be they don't know that much about your company. It might be the guarantee. You write them down. Then you simply say, "Are these the only objections?" You deal with them one at a time, and as you do, you simply say, "Is that a satisfactory answer to your question?" Then you cross them out. "Does that clarify the issue to your satisfaction?" would be another way of putting it.

When you have them all crossed out, then subliminally you have said, "I've eliminated any reason for you not owning the product. Therefore you in essence have said, 'I want to go ahead and do business with you.'"

As salespeople, we need to understand this: the prospect wants to say yes. I know that might surprise some of you, especially if you've had a half-dozen nos in a row. They really do want to say yes. One reason is that *no* is so final. You know, there's something about us people that makes us want to not totally terminate any relationship unless it is a bad one. If you've been acting in a professional manner, they really do want to say yes.

There's a second reason why they want to say yes: if they don't say yes to you, and if there's a need for this or a similar product, they're going to have to talk to another salesperson. In our company, for example, a lot of times we have certain needs, and I know that on occasion we have bought although we had not had all of our objections answered. But we had looked and looked to find. The comment would be made, "Well, we would have to go through it again."

They really do want to do business. Most of your prospects do. They want to say yes.

Some objections that you encounter are better to answer later. You might be demonstrating one feature, and they ask something entirely unrelated. If you can answer it in one word, I would suggest you go ahead and do it, even if it's just a sentence or so, except when they bring up price. It might not be appropriate to answer that right at that moment.

But if you don't want to handle the objection at that point, simply say, "You know, that's a very exciting feature of our product. You are going to be delighted when I get to that point, but if you don't mind, let me pursue this, because we're at such a critical area that I need to tie some things together which are very relevant, but I promise to get back to it. If I neglect to do that, would you remind me? Don't you forget." As a matter of fact, if you're wise on your talking pad, you will scratch a little note so they can see that you're not trying to put them off, that you really do want to answer them.

Now you need to plan ahead. You should memorize a lot of ways to say the same thing. If you do, you will come to realize there are a lot of ways to say the same thing, but there's only one way to say it the best. Find out what that best way is and stay with it.

Again, when they bring up the objection you do not want to answer right then, you act pleased. You get permission to delay: "If you don't mind, I'd like to answer that question in a moment, and I promise to do exactly that." Keep that promise. Then you close that little bit down by saying, "Is that fair enough?" Everybody basically wants to be fair, so when you say, "Is that fair enough?" they give you permission.

Some objections are not meant to be answered, so you just kind of smile and ignore them, but if the question comes up again, regardless of how absurd it sounds, you then deal with it.

Here's something we need to understand. You're not in the sales-answering-objection business. You're in the sales business. I have been on calls on many occasions where I was training another salesperson, and I would watch that salesperson answer an objection. Then they would, in essence, fold their arms and say, "Well, I handled that pretty good. Go ahead, shoot another one at me. I'll take care of it too. Go ahead, challenge me." That's crazy. You answer the objections, then you close.

Sometimes selling involves simple little analogies, or it involves just asking for the order. I'm thinking of a friend of mine named Randy Cooper up in Enid, Oklahoma. He runs a furniture store. Randy told me that he'd been listening to our tapes, and he'd been able to translate a couple of my examples and utilize them, with slight alterations, to fit his business perfectly.

He was telling me about this lady who came in for a reclining chair. Her husband was getting it for her as a Christmas present, and he sent her down to the store to pick it out. She had brought her teenaged daughter along with her, found exactly the chair she wanted. It was $449.95. She loved it, and she said to Randy, "I'll go home and talk to my husband."

Randy said, "You know, I have two children, and I keep them three and four days a week. My grocery bill runs about $100 a week."

The lady said, "There are three of us, and that's about what my grocery bill runs."

"You know," Randy said, "I'd almost bet you that you never really talk to your husband about that grocery bill. You just go ahead and buy the groceries, don't you?"

"Yes."

"Interestingly, $100 a week is over $5000 a year. You never ask your husband about the $5000. He's anxious for you to have this. He's giving it to you. Do you really want to go home and talk to him about it?"

Randy said the lady looked down at her teenaged daughter and said, "I'll take it." A simple, little analogy which she could relate to.

Often people don't get the order because they don't ask for it. Randy was sharing with me that this couple had been in to refurnish their home. They had been married a number of years. The kids were now grown to the degree that they wouldn't destroy the furniture any longer, so the order was significant, and the bill was substantial. When Randy presented the total, the lady said, "Ooh, that is a lot of money. We'll go home and talk about this."

Randy acted as if he had not heard a word that she said. He looked at the husband and said, "Let me ask you this question. When you get this, are you going to want to haul it home yourself, or will you want me to deliver it?"

The man turned to his wife, and said, "What do you think?"

Remember that ten seconds earlier she had said, "We'll go home and think about it," but when the husband said, "What do you think?" she vehemently answered, "Shucks, no. He charges money to deliver that stuff. We'll just take it home ourselves." Ask for the order.

Let's take a quick look at three different kinds of prospects. First of all, there's Gary Gullible. You deal with old Gary in an open, straightforward way. Tell him lots of human-interest stories. He's more likely to buy because he likes and trusts you than for any other reason. He responds to persuasion but is offended with speed and pressure. Deal with him gently but confidently.

Then there's the other end of the spectrum. There's old Sidney Skeptical. The skeptical, antagonistic prospect wants to be right, and he wants to be understood. When he raises a dogmatic objection with a little anger, cynicism, or sarcasm hidden underneath it, you should respond by saying, "I'm delighted you raised that question, Mr. Prospect. To make absolutely certain I clearly understand what you're saying, would you mind repeating it?"

This does a couple of things. First of all, it indicates an honest effort on your part to be fair, and it also indicates that you place considerable importance on what the prospect is saying. Additionally, when he repeats his objection, chances are good he will substantially reduce the tone of that objection.

I've had that happen to me a thousand times in my sales career. Somebody will be dogmatic, sarcastic, even antagonistic in their objection. I'd say, "I appreciate your position, but to make really certain I understand it, would you mind repeating it?" It's astonishing how much softer it comes out the second time. You can deal with it far more effectively.

In dealing with skeptical, antagonistic prospects, it's important not to argue or contradict what they're saying, even if they're wrong. Let them finish saying what they have to say. Get it off their chest, blow off that steam. Once that is out of their system and they've seen that you're concerned about them, your chances of penetrating their minds and closing the sale are increased substantially.

There's old Ivan Indecisive. You know about Ivan, who wanted to start a procrastinators' club but decided to wait until later. Ivan simply cannot make a decision. He takes a pep pill to get charged up to do something and then mixes it with Valium, so if nothing happens, it won't bother him.

The way to deal with him is to win his confidence, which you do by being the right kind of person. Demonstrate considerable empathy, move to his side of the table, and let him know you're on his side. Reassure him that yes, he is making the right move. Your own conviction and belief that your product is what he should buy will be the determining factor. Remember, he's having trouble deciding if he should buy. If you have any doubts that you should sell, you can rest assured that he won't buy. Push him. Be firm.

The sales professional is one who understands very thoroughly that he can have all the prospects he wants. He can get all the appointments he wants. He can make all the presentations he wants, but until he takes advantage and capitalizes on closing opportunities, he is never going to be successful in the world of selling.

I've had it said so many times by a lot of salespeople. They come to me and say, "You know, I can do everything but close. I know how to get prospects. I know how to set up appointments. I know how to handle objections. I can do everything but close."

What they're really saying is, "I don't know how to sell," because until you close, you're nothing but a conversationalist. You need to know how to handle these objections and use them as a closing opportunity.

One secret of successful selling is that the professional is always on the grow. Be a pro and grow. That's important for building a sales career.

10

The Power of Voice Inflection

Zig

I do not exaggerate with this statement: any salesperson today who does not have their own cassette recorder has not fully gotten into the profession of selling. I cannot conceive of a salesperson who does not have their own recorder-player.

If you record your presentation, it will make a substantial difference in your productivity. If it is possible with all of the fancy little mics nowadays, have somebody out in the car or in another office recording your talk while you're presenting to a prospect.

If you can't do it that way, then by all means get in a training situation and record your entire presentation. Record the way you handle objections. Record the way you make the appointment. Record the way you do everything in the process of selling, and here's what you're going to discover.

You're going to discover that what you say and what you tell your sales manager that you've been saying are two entirely different things. I'm going to suggest that you take that recording and script it. As you write out what you have recorded, you're going to be astonished at some of the things you discover.

For example, you're probably going to discover that you talk too much. That's one of the things that a lot of people are a little shocked at. The second thing you'll discover is that you often hear what the prospect say but are missing what that prospect is saying.

You often give non-answers to objections and miss a lot of closing opportunities. You and/or the prospect will often go off on tangents which are absolutely incredible. In long interviews, here's what you discover: You get into a monotone. Your enthusiasm begins to die, and it really does make a difference in effectiveness.

I know what a lot of people say: "Now, wait a minute, Ziglar. The way I sound on recording and the way I really sound is not exactly the same." Oh, I have news for you. It really is.

When you yourself listen to what you say, it sounds different, because the sound is literally coming through bone. Now I'm not calling you a bonehead; I'm just saying it comes through bone. When you record what you say, it comes back through the air, and that's where the difference comes in.

I'm going to suggest that first of all you record one sentence: "I did not say he stole the money." This is eight simple words, but when you use your voice properly, that simple sentence can say eight entirely different things. You need to record the sentence until your friend or your wife or husband or your manager can clearly identify all eight of the things that it's saying.

First of all, "I did not say he stole the money" is simply a statement of fact, but by changing the inflection you can make it say something different. "I did *not* say he stole the money." Totally different. Or "I did not *say* he stole the money." I'll admit it, I implied it, but I sure didn't say it. Or "I did not say *he* stole the money." That's the rascal who got the money right over there. Or "I did not say he *stole* the money." He was going to put it back in a couple of years. I mean, he just was borrowing it. "I did not say he stole *the* money." It was this other money over here. Or "I did not say he stole the *money*." The rascal got her jewels, that's what it was.

The way you say what you say does make a difference. Now let's look at your inflection as it relates to price. Have you, for example, ever had somebody say, "Well, your price is a little out

Now in "Secrets of Closing the Sale," and in our audio series, we spend ninety minutes on voice inflection as it relates to price. Price alone. That's kind of like hitting a fly with a sledgehammer, but when we get through, that sucker's dead, I guarantee it. He's gone. We don't deal with him anymore.

Different prospects will give you that price objection in different ways. Sometimes a prospect says,

"That price is ridiculous." That's pretty strong, isn't it? Others say, "Well, the price is a little high." When they give you the objections with different tones of voice, you really do have a different situation. You do not handle them in exactly the same way.

When a person says, "That price is ridiculous," you repeat what they said. You lower your voice, you look them right in the eye and simply say, "The price is ridiculous?" That sounds so simple, but I can guarantee you, you will have to hear that a number of times, and you will have to practice it on your recorder a number of times before you get it exactly right.

What I did was very simple: I moved the objection back to the prospect's side of the table. Now the prospect has to defend his statement versus your having to justify the price. There's a dramatic difference in the results.

Ladies, you'll be delighted to know that this works beautifully at home. For example, you might have had a tough day at the office or at home. You're home when you husband gets in, and as he walks in, you of course greet him warmly and affectionately; that's standard operating procedure. Then, when he recovers, you look at him and say, "Honey, did you want to take me to Farfallo's or Papillon's for dinner this evening?"

Now he might have had a tough day too. He might look right back at you and say, "I don't want to take you anywhere to dinner." You don't argue with him.

You just lower your voice and say, "You don't want to take me to dinner?" It almost ain't fair, I'll tell you.

Voice inflection—we use it everywhere. For example, it might be grass-cutting time, and you might say to your son, "OK, son. Time to cut the grass." That sixteen-year-old might say, "I don't want to cut the grass." You just look at him and say, "You don't want to cut the grass, son?" It is absolutely astonishing, the difference in effectiveness when you use that approach.

It might be time for your son to start doing his lessons, so you say, "OK, son, time to cut the TV off and get your lessons." He might say, "I don't want to get my lessons." You lower your voice, you look right at him and say, "You don't want an education, son?" A lady the other night said, "Won't that make him feel guilty?" I said, "Yes."

I don't know where we got the insane idea that we're never supposed to feel any guilt. Did you know that if there weren't guilt feelings, we would have license to rob, murder, rape, steal, kill, do everything? A little guilt is not a bad thing to have. It's a must if we're going to stay in a civilized society.

Once in a while, you'll have a prospect who will look at you and say, "It seems to me that price is a little high." You might simply look at him and say, "Let me ask you, Mr. Prospect, every once in a while, don't you think you deserve something that is just a little high?"

It's amazing what something like that will do. Why not treat yourself once in a while? You deserve it.

Another prospect might say, "It seems to me that the price is a little high" when you have a very limited amount of time. One of the most effective, one of the most powerful closes I think I have seen yet is this one. You simply lower your voice as you look at the prospect and say, "Well, you know, Mr. Prospect, many years ago our company made a basic decision. We decided that it would be easier to explain price one time than it would be to apologize for quality forever. I'll bet you're glad we made that decision, aren't you?"

Does that sort of thing work in the real world? Ab Jackson, an insurance representative in Tucson, Arizona, said to me, "Zig, one night I was on my way to the biggest sales opportunity I'd ever had. The proposal I had, if the prospect bought, was worth twice as many dollars in business as any contract I'd ever written. But I was really dragging bottom. I was listening to this recording of yours on my way out, and I heard those words. I got down to the close after I'd made the proposal, and the prospect dogmatically said, 'That price is too high.'

"I did almost it with a little twist at the end," which you have to do in sales; you have to alter the situation a little to fit your specific need. Ab Jackson lowered his voice. "I looked the prospect right in the eye and said, 'Mr. Prospect, many years ago, the founders of this company made a very important decision. They decided that it would be easier to explain the price one time than it would be to have to apologize for lack of service on claims and benefits forever. Deep down, Mr. Prospect, I have an idea that you're delighted that they made that decision.'" Ab said he got awfully quiet for a few seconds. Then the man said, "You're right. I'll take it."

The right words, the right intentions, the right voice inflection, the right concept behind you will really make a major difference. Sometimes, however, after you've answered one, two, three, four objections, the prospect might say, "It doesn't make any difference what I bring up. You have an answer for everything."

At that particular point, you're that close to making the sale, or you're that close to missing it. What you say and the way you say it is going to make the difference. If you modestly admit after a compliment like that that you were number one in the region that month and the month before, then you have just fed your ego. That's really all that's going to happen.

If you want to make the sale, if you want to get *you* out of the way and let your product and your persuasive ability take over so that you can benefit that prospect by selling them, then you lower your voice, you look him right in the eye, and you say, "I really appreciate that, and I'm going to take it as a sincere compliment, but the truth is there are many questions I do not have the answer for. That's one reason I'm so excited about selling the product, which is the answer to your needs, and that's really what you want, isn't it?"

I'll say it again. The right product, the right words, the proper inflection, and most importantly, the right intent, and you have a successful, professional salesperson.

I'd like to share an example of how this can be put together in an effective presentation. About ten years ago, I was passing through St. Louis, Missouri. I had a little time to invest, and so I was down at the carousel close to where the shoe-shine stand is, and I needed a shine, so I walked up to the little area there where they shine shoes, a very small room.

All four of the guys in there shining shoes were busy. There were no more chairs, so I stood at the entranceway. In a couple of minutes, the young man in the third chair finished shining, and his prospect put his paper down as he climbed out of the chair.

The young man pointed to me and said, "You're next." I climbed up in the chair and sat down. The young shoe shiner finished the cash transaction with his customer, and while he was doing that, I was looking at the prices. At that time, the regular shine was 75 cents, the wax shine was $1, and the spit shine was $2. I looked at it carefully and said, "I'll get the 75-cent shine, tip the guy a quarter, and I'll be on my way."

The young man, whose name was Johnny—I know, because he had his nametag on—came over and looked at me, and he said, "What kind?"

I said, "I'll take the regular."

He took a step backward, looked up at me, and said, "Regular?" Should have known then I was in for an unusual shoe shine, but I wasn't about to let that dude get the best of me, so I said, "Yes, you guys do such a fantastic job, and I'll be on my way in a matter of minutes."

He never said a thing, never even grunted. He just reached over and he got the saddle soap to clean the shoes with, and he quickly put that all over both shoes. Then he took the drying cloth and dried my left shoe. As soon as he finished drying it, he ran his fingers over the leather, and he had them squeaky clean. You could hear them squeak from a block off. He said, "Man, these are really nice shoes."

I said, "Thank you very much."

"They're Ballys, aren't they?"

"As a matter of fact, they are." He said, "Don't they cost a lot of money?" I said, "Oh, brother, do they ever cost a lot of money, but I do a lot of work on my feet, and I really need comfortable shoes."

"I bet they are comfortable, aren't they?"

"They are really a comfortable pair of shoes."

By then, he had finished drying the shoes off, and he reached over to get the polish to put on them, but before he did, he reached up and he grabbed my pant leg, and he said, "That is the most unusual piece of cloth I think I have ever felt."

It is an unusual cloth. My good friend Doyle Hoyer from Fort Madison, Iowa, who sells me my clothes, says this cloth comes from Ireland. He guarantees it's going to last me at least five years. I believe it will, because I've already been wearing it a couple of years, and I can't even tell that it's not a brand-new suit.

Johnny said, "What kind of suit is it?"

"It's a Hickey-Freeman."

"Man," he said, "those dudes do cost money."

"Yes, they're not inexpensive. The cloth on this one made it especially expensive, but I'm convinced I have a real good buy." I ended up wearing that suit nearly ten years. I had the lapels altered so it fit, and after about eight years, I put a new lining in it, but other than that, it was a beautiful suit all of that length of time. I was sharing how sold I was on the suit, and he was shining away.

I don't know how much you know about shoe shining, but let me give you one little basic fact about it. When you hear that cloth popping, that popping has nothing whatever to do with the shining. That is merchandising. That is sales talk, and I'm in favor of that. All the way, I'm in favor of it. He's trying to attract a crowd from outside to come in and see what's going on.

Well, he was just a-shining and a-popping. All of a sudden, between pops he stopped, he backed away, he looked right into my eyes and said, "You know, it just seems like a shame. A man will spend over $100 on a pair of shoes. He'll spend several hundred dollars on a suit of clothes, and all he's trying to do is look his best. Then he won't spend another dollar to get the best-looking shoe shine in the whole world to top all the rest of it off."

I said, "Spit on them, man, spit on them."

Now I don't know how you are, but when I get a 75-cent shine, a two-bit tip is all right, but who ever heard of a two-bit tip on a $2 shine? Folks with class just don't do things like that, so I took a dollar to go with the two, and I handed it to him, and man, I go walking out of there. You're talking about a high-stepper. Old Zig is picking him up and putting them down, thinking, "What in the world is this guy doing shining shoes?"

Then I looked up at the clock, and the clock showed straight up and down 10:00. It clicked as I looked. When I sat down, it had clicked three minutes to 10:00. I was in his chair three minutes. I gave him $3. Now, you do not have to be a Phi Beta Kappa from MIT to figure that one out. That is $60 an hour. That is $480 a day.

I know what you're thinking: "Yes, but, Ziglar, you and me both know that he doesn't make $480 a day." I know that. Cut in half in two. Make it $240. Cut that half in two. Make it $120. Cut that half in two. Make it $60; $60 a day figures out to be over $18,000 a year, but I guarantee you that dude is making over $30,000 a year shining shoes. He's good. He's real good, but let's not get confused here.

The reason he's doing that is, number one, he is a professional salesperson, one of the best I have ever seen. He's good. He goes out after business. When things are slack at his stand, he goes out into an area

100 feet away, and he starts bringing people in. He delivers what he sells. When he sells that shoe shine, he delivers every bit of it.

You know, I personally believe our rate of divorce would decline about 95 percent if we delivered in marriage what we sell in courtship. I believe our sales careers would catapult forward if we would deliver everything that we sell, keep our promises.

Johnny was a professional. He's the only shoe shiner I have ever seen who had a name tag. It just had "Johnny." I asked him his last name. He said, "I'm not going to tell you. If I do, you'll forget them both, but you'll never forget Johnny." He also had a title: shoe-ologist.

There's a sequel to this story. I was back in there a couple of years later. I walked by the stand. There was nobody else there, not another customer, not another guy shining shoes. I walked in, I hung up my bag, and Johnny said, "Have a seat."

When I sat down, I noticed they'd changed the prices. A regular shine was $1. They no longer had the wax shine, and they changed the name of the spit shine to the best shine, so when I sat down, he said, "What kind?"

Well, I didn't want to go through that again, so I said, "Give me the best."

I found out a long time ago that people work better with praise than any other way, so I started expressing my appreciation for Johnny as a professional. I said how good he was and how wonderful it was to see somebody enthused about their work and to take such pride in it. He acknowledged those compliments, and since nobody else was there, he just kept shining. He'd put the polish on and shine, he'd put it on and shine. Finally I had to say, "Johnny, I'll tell you, I have to go."

So he finished up, beautifully, and as I stepped down he said, "You know, you've been asking me a lot of questions. Do you mind if I ask you a couple of questions?"

I said, "No. Go right ahead."

"I can't help but notice that you have hung an overnight bag there."

I said, "Yes."

"Does that mean you're going to spend the night in St. Louis?"

"Yes, I am."

He said, "Do you, by any chance, have another pair of shoes in that bag?"

"Well, as a matter of fact, I do."

"You know, it'd really be a shame to have the best-looking shoe shine in St. Louis tonight and look like one of the guys tomorrow. It won't take me but a minute, and you'll be on your way." I left $5 with that dude that time.

Do you believe I was upset when he wanted to shine my other pair of shoes, or do you believe I was tickled and delighted that he had asked for the business in the way that indicated that he wanted me to look good to the public?

There are some significant lessons we can learn from this story. Number one, Johnny honestly believes he's the best shoe shiner on the face of this earth. If you don't believe it, you just ask him. He'll say, "None better than me, man, nobody is better." Incidentally, his stand now is under the restaurant, and so when you go into that airport, go there, and get that shine from Johnny.

The second lesson that he can teach us is the fact that he believes in his product. His own shoes were shined to a standstill. He was representative of what he was selling. When you looked at his shoes, you would think to yourself, "Boy, that's the way I want my shoes to look."

Number three—a lesson us sales professionals can learn—is he was a hard worker. When business slacks, as I indicated earlier, he goes after it, but when he is shining, he is really working at those shoes. Number four, he's enthusiastic. All of us love to be around enthusiastic people.

Number five, he's adaptable. On my first exposure to Johnny, he was shining a guy who was sitting there reading the paper, obviously interested only in reading his paper. Johnny said nothing to him. He let the guy do what he wanted to do. He let him read his paper. He talked to me because it was obvious I wanted to talk.

Number six, Johnny asked the prospect to buy. I'll tell you that is significant. And the seventh lesson—

he doesn't hesitate to upgrade and add to what they already are buying.

The truth is very simple, and most of us would fit in this category: we're calling on customers whom we've dealt with in the past who are currently buying from us. We have additional products to sell, and yet for whatever reason, for fear we're going to be considered pushy, or for fear that we might lose the business we already have, we are not offering the additional services.

Don't misunderstand that. I don't believe every salesperson should offer every prospect or every customer everything they sell every time they go in there. But I do believe that on a regular basis, you should come in with an additional product you're excited about, which you know your customer is buying from someone else, and give them an opportunity to consolidate their orders with you.

It's not a question of selling them something they neither want nor need. You are offering them something they're already buying, maybe of a lesser quality at a higher price from someone else. Yes, you are servicing the account. You're doing what the professional ought to be doing.

The professional is truly a well-balanced person, one that looks at all phases of selling. This professional has integrity, he's knowledgeable, and he's aggressively caring in his creative approach to solving the problems of the prospect, whether that is a shoe shine they're in need of, cosmetic dentistry they might have a use for, magnificent transportation they must have, a computer program, or an investment approach to life that makes sense. The professional does it with integrity and persistence and with the customer's best interest at heart. That's the sign of the professional salesperson. That's really what successful selling is all about.

11

CHAPTER

The Keys to Successful Selling, Part 1

Zig

I'd like to start with four major points. I want to cover these before we look at the keys in selling. Number one, there never has been, there never will be, in my opinion, a outstanding salesperson, one who went all the way to the top, who was a leader. There's never been a truly outstanding salesperson who was normal.

In every instance, they're a little bit warped in their belief in what they're selling. They cannot imagine anybody not saying, "Yes, I'll take it," and because they cannot imagine anybody not buying, by the very force of their own conviction and attitude they do end up winning those close ones. The professional wins the close ones, and when I say "wins," I mean that he helps the prospect to win through the ownership of the product.

The problem with this is that a lot of times when you get so wrapped up in something and you believe in it so strongly and somebody still says no, there's a chance you might confuse their business refusal, which is all it is, with a personal rejection, which it is not.

My son, for example, understood that completely almost from birth. He would ask me for something, and I would say no. He wouldn't get upset. He just figured that old Dad had missed the question. He would wait a few minutes and then give me a chance to correct an obvious mistake.

The third point is that you have to remember who wins. If you are a professional, you understand that it is the prospect who is going to be the big winner. I say "if you're a professional" because the professional would sell only those things which would benefit the prospect in the long run, satisfying some need which is greater than the price of whatever you're selling.

The fourth thing I want to emphasize is that there is no such thing as a natural-born salesman. I've been virtually all over this world of ours. I have seen where women have given birth to boys, I've seen where they've given birth to girls, but thus far I have never yet seen where a woman has given birth to a salesperson. Now I also read where salespeople die, so if they're not born, but they do die, then somewhere between birth and death, by choice and by training, they become professional salespeople.

With those four points behind us, let's look at some of the keys which will be enormously helpful to you in your sales career. The first key we want to look at is what we call *the key of positive projection.*

Your business is never either good or bad *out there.* Your business is either good or bad right here between your ears. If your thinking is good, your business is going to be good, but if your thinking is stinking, then your business is not going to be so good.

One of my favorite stories took place a number of years ago. As a matter of fact, I heard this story over thirty years ago. So it's not brand-new, but it is so beautiful and emphasizes and illustrates what I want to say so completely that I share it with you.

This printing company had an expansion program under way. They were hiring a new salesperson every six months. They would train this person in the office. Then they would train this individual out in the field with an experienced salesman. Just before the new salesperson went out on his first call, the boss would call him in for that extra little pep talk.

On this one occasion, they hired an unusually young salesman, and he looked ever younger than he really was. He appeared to be scared to death. So the boss called him in and said, "Son, let me put your mind at ease. I'm going to send you right across the street to call on an account. Let me warn you in advance: that's one of the meanest, nastiest, orneriest, most foul-mouthed old goats on the face of this earth. He's going to make you think he's going to bite your head off and chew it up and spit it out in little bitty pieces but, son, he's all bark. He is no bite. Inside, he is soft as mush. All you have to do is hang in there and somewhere along the way let him know that you're a brand-new salesman. I guarantee you he will do for you as he always does. He always buys something—not much, but he always buys something."

Armed with this information, our young hero went across the street on this first significant sales call of his career. He enthusiastically walked in and introduced himself to the prospect, and that's the last thing he said for about ten minutes. That old boy really read him the riot act. He told him how the cow ate the cabbage in no uncertain terms. He introduced him to a segment of the English language that the young man never knew existed.

It didn't faze our hero even a little bit. He just stood his ground, and when the old boy finally got through chewing, he came right back at him: "Yes, sir, I know and I understand all of that, and I appreciate your position, but we now have the finest printing offer and the finest printing in this entire city. We are prepared now to offer you something that has never been available to you before."

They went back and forth for about thirty minutes. Finally, the young man got his sale, and it wasn't just a little old piddly-wink order. It was the biggest order in the history of the company. He was understandably excited. I mean, he was enthused. He was turned on. He ran back across the street to the boss, threw the order down on his desk, and said, "Oh, boy, were you ever right. That old buzzard really is a foul-mouthed old goat. He's mean, and he's nasty, and he's ornery, but you were sure right when you said he was a buyer. Look, I have the biggest order in the company's history."

The boss took one look at it and said, "Oh my goodness, son, you've called on the wrong man. I told you to go next door. That old buzzard is the meanest, nastiest, orneriest, most foul-mouthed, old goat in this town. We have been trying for years and years to sell to him. You're the first one to scratch an order pad with him." It's a true story.

My question is this: where did he make the sale? Did he make the sale in the office, or did he simply go across to write the order? You know the answer better than I. You know perfectly good and well he had made the sale before he ever left his office.

The first thing we need to understand in this key of positive projection is, as professionals, we need to make that sale before we encounter the prospect. That's true whether we're in a retail business, where they come to see us, or whether we're in a business where we go out to see the prospect. It doesn't make any difference about the location. The needs of the prospect are the same, and we need to have our thinking properly adjusted.

The second key I'd like to share with you is what I call the *key of the assumptive attitude.* We need to zero in on that, because much of what selling really is all about has to do with our attitude.

I'll never forget the day in my neighborhood three years ago when I was out doing my jogging. It was that afternoon, and I was 99 percent through with my jog. As I circled the block one last time to come by the house, I noticed a young man talking to the redhead there in the front door of our home.

They were so intent in their conversation that I figured this must be pretty serious. So I decided to abort my run, and I walked over. The young man stuck his hand out, and he said, "Mr. Ziglar, I'm Tom Brickman, and I was just doing a little work here in the neighborhood. I'm trying to find some pool owners who would like to reduce the cost of their chemicals by at least 50 percent and cut down on their work in keeping their pool clean to the degree that they only have to invest about ten minutes to have the most beautiful pool in the neighborhood. I'm just wondering, Mr. Ziglar, if I have just described you."

Man, what are you going to say? You have to say that that young man has a powerful opening there, and if I'm going to be honest, I have to admit I'm interested in cutting my cost. I'm interested in reducing my work. So I grinned. I love salespeople anyhow.

"Tom," I said, "you've hit the jackpot. That's exactly what I'm looking for."

He said, "We're cleaning pools in the neighborhood absolutely free of charge. We're demonstrating a magnificent new robot. It's a Creepy Crawly. It's just been invented and perfected and put on the market. An engineer who got tired of all the trouble of cleaning his pools came up with it, and it's absolutely fabulous. We will simply put it in your pool, and you'll see the most amazing sight."

"I sure don't like the one I have," I said, "so let's have a peek."

We made the appointment, he came back, we went out to the swimming pool, and he unpacked a brand-new Creepy Crawly. The assumption is obvious, isn't it? He's going to leave that one in the pool. He starts out with that particular thing. He showed me exactly how to install it.

He said, "Now here's all you do with your Creepy," and he started talking about Creepy like it was a person. Creepy this, and Creepy that. He had really personalized it. "You put your Creepy here, and you do this with your Creepy, and you watch Creepy work." It was absolutely fabulous what he was doing.

He kept emphasizing the point that there's only one moving part, and as old Creepy went to work, I was impressed. I'll tell you, it did a good job. After it had been in the pool for about fifteen minutes, with Tom telling me all of the little things to go along with it, he reached over and got his talking pad out, and he said, "Now, Mr. Ziglar, one of the beautiful things about Creepy is this. We are going to have a design of your swimming pool in our service department. I want to draw the design exactly with all of the details filled in. The reason that's so important," he said as he was sketching the outline, "is that if you ever have any difficulty, if Creepy is not cleaning a certain area of the pool, all you have to do is get on the telephone and tell us exactly where it is. With your design, we will know exactly what to do. In 98 percent of the cases, you won't even have to have a service call."

He said, "Now I have it with these dimensions. Does this look like an accurate picture of your pool?" Notice how he's getting me involved in the whole thing?

I said, "Yes, Tom, you're a pretty good artist. That's exactly the way the pool looks. The dimensions are exactly right."

"What do you think about the job Creepy is doing? Notice wherever he goes it's cleaning? You can see the difference, can't you, Mr. Ziglar?" He never said the rest of it was dirty; he said, "You can see the difference."

"Yes, it's doing a good job."

Then he assumed again. He said, "Now, Mr. Ziglar, obviously this is a brand-new Creepy Crawly. I just took it out of the box, you saw it, but since it has been working a few minutes now, if you would prefer, I will get another one out of another box and put it in. Which would you prefer?"

He's given me an alternative choice. I said, "Well, Tom, this one's brand-new, and I know it works. I don't know that that new one out of the box would. This one's fine."

Along with his talking pad was his order pad, and he said, "Now you can handle this either with a check or a credit card. Which would you prefer?"

"The redhead will just give you a check for it. I'd prefer it that way."

It was that simple. Textbook example. I had a need, he had a product. He was a professional sales-man who believed in what he was selling. He demon-strated effectively. He led me through all of the steps, and when you have a good person selling a good product, it is almost impossible to resist if you have the need, the desire, and the money to purchase.

There's something else about Tom which I believe is very important. As you noticed, he asked an awful lot of questions. He had an assumptive attitude from hello to good-bye. He gave me the alternative choice all the way.

The next key, which is so important, is called the *key of physical action*. I'm a little embarrassed to have to say what I'm going to say. First thing, you need to be clean. I know that I ought not to have to say a thing like that to professionals, but you can't believe the number of salespeople who do not take a bath or a shower before they go out to greet the pub-lic. They do not use any deodorant. We need to be smelling good.

I'm not talking about overdoing it. I'm not talking about having so much cologne or aftershave on that you can be smelled coming a block away, and certainly not an overabundance of those beautiful perfumes which are available, but you need to smell clean and fresh.

You need to be properly dressed to sell. What is proper dress? That's going to vary with the area, with the product, and with your personality. There are a lot of good books on proper ways to dress. My own concept is this: you should be dressed in such a way that the people you're dealing with almost do not notice that you have on the clothes you're wearing. If you leave here saying, "Man, did you see that gorgeous suit that dude had on?" I will have failed. If you leave here saying, "Boy, you'd have thought he could have done better than that, wouldn't you?" I definitely will have failed. Dress properly.

Now, ladies, this is a little delicate, but let me put it this way: If you dress in such a way that you get that male prospect so shook up that he doesn't know whether he's coming or going, that's like shooting a bird on the ground. That is not fair, but of infinitely more significance, it is not professional, and you will never really build a career. Your rate of cancellation will be high. Your repeat business will definitely be down. You will encounter all kinds of difficulties. It is not professional. You just don't do it.

When I talk about physical action, I'm also talking about learning something about body language. Since this is such a significant subject, I just want to tell you about four very simple little things, but they can make a significant difference in your career. I call it the CHEF method, C-H-E-F.

C: when you've offered them a product, or you are demonstrating and you see them stroking their cheek or their chin, that's a reflective sign. They are assuming ownership. They are visualizing what it will mean. H: When you see their hands, particularly rubbing together, whether it's palm against palm or palm against the back of the hand, they are assuming ownership in their mind.

E: when you look at their eyes, and their eyes begin to open wider, and you can see that little light start to shine—particularly if they're an older person and they have a few crow's-feet, when those crow's-feet begin to relax—you watch that. They are buying what you are selling.

The F is for *friendly*. When the prospect says to you, "Why you rascal, old Jesse James used a gun to get my money, and here you are coming in with this beautiful product and a pen and paper to get my money," you know that you're in the process of making the sale.

Physical action also means that you have come prepared to sell. Your products are there, your kit is in neat order, and your demonstration material is handy. You have gotten the order book out with all the other stuff. You're prepared to sell, and you're in position to sell.

Also, if you're a salesman and you're dealing with a man and his wife, don't sit too close to the wife. If you accidentally or deliberately touch the wife, you're not going to sell that man anything—guaranteed. Jealousy does rear its head. Be careful about where you sit.

It's also important that the man have the wife next to him, because we often have a tendency to ignore members of the opposite sex in a presentation. The salesperson might bypass the wife and talk too much to the husband, but the wife might be the one who makes the decision. The husband needs to have her next to him so that she's included in the entire process.

If it's reversed, and we have a saleslady calling on this man and his wife, then we need the saleslady next to the man for exactly the same reason, but again, not that close. Physical action, your position, is important.

If it's possible to have your prospects seated when you are closing the sale, particularly if it is a major purchase, then you can do it more effectively. People are more comfortable on their seats than they are on their feet.

Physical action might mean something as simple as this: if you're touring in real estate, and you pick up the man and his wife to take them out, when they first get in the car, you have the contracts with you. You simply have them there.

You hand them either to the man or his wife and say, "In this part of the country, this is the standard information which we use, and the standard forms which we go by if you happen to find what you really want." From the moment they have started there, you've let it be known that there is an agreement involved, and you get it out early. That eliminates a lot of the difficulty later on. The contract is not something you suddenly whip out and let them see. It's something that they understand is one of the forms you use around here. Yes, physical action is important.

The fourth key I want to share with you is what we call the *key of enthusiasm*. It's easily the most misunderstood key of all, because a lot of people seem to think that enthusiasm means that you're loud and wild and way over the place. Some of the most enthusiastic people I've ever seen are very quiet, introverted people, but as you talk to them you sense the intensity of their belief, their conviction. *Enthusiasm* comes from two Greek words, *en theos*, and it means *God within*.

If you look at the word *enthusiasm*, you will notice that the last four letters are I-A-S-M. That forms an acrostic for I Am Sold Myself. When you are sold yourself, yes, it really will and does make a difference.

From time to time, I've had salespeople ask me if you can be too enthusiastic. Well, I'd like to share with you a story. Many years ago, a young fellow was courting his girlfriend, and they lived out in the rural areas. This was before everybody had automobiles. He was working there on the farm, and he finished a little late. By the time he got cleaned up to head to his girlfriend's house, he was running late.

He knew if he was much later, that girl would not go out with him, but since he did not have a car, the only way he could get there any sooner was to take a shortcut across the pasture. That had a problem. There were 1200 pounds of big, bad bull in that pasture. The young man evaluated his situation, finally decided that the prize was worth the risk, and started to cross the pasture.

He was jogging along a little easily; he did not want to attract too much attention, but he did not want to stay in that pasture any longer than he had to. He got about a third of the way across when all of the sudden he heard the thundering hoofbeats of 1200 pounds of big, bad, and now very mad bull.

Our hero shifted into high gear. He was doing the hundred in about six-eight, but the bull was doing it in about five-two. That bull was gaining at every step. He got so close that the young man could feel the bull's breath on his feet.

I don't know if you have ever felt bull breath on your heels or not, but the young man was in a desperate situation. He looked around for help. The only thing he could see straight ahead was a tree, but it only had one limb, and it was twenty-two feet up in the air. He gave another burst of energy. He got within jumping distance, and he made a mighty leap for the limb, but he missed it. Fortunately, he caught it coming down.

With enthusiasm, you might miss some sales, but you have a good chance of catching them when you come down. For every sale you miss because you're too enthusiastic, you'll miss fifteen because you're not enthusiastic enough. Those are the odds that I like to use.

Now let's look at the next one, which is the *key of the subordinate question*. What is a subordinate question? It's any question the answer to which, if positive, means they've bought, but if it is negative, it does not mean they have not bought.

For example, my friend Hal Krause uses this one. "Mr. Prospect, have you sold yourself?" (You don't ever ask, "Have I sold you?") "Have you sold yourself, or should I tell you some more?" Well, if the guy has sold himself, then you obviously write the order, but if they say, "No, I need to learn, I need a little more information before I make a decision," then that's really all a good salesperson asks. A subordinate question could be a trial close.

For example, "If these tires give your family the extra protection they'd certainly be worth the extra four cents a day, wouldn't they?" Then there's the old and familiar three-question close: "Can you see where this would save you some money?" Understand that this is after you've demonstrated. "Are you interested in saving money? If you were ever going to start saving money, when do you think would be the time to start?"

You might be selling a health-related item. "Can you see where this would be better for your health?

Are you interested in taking care of your health? If you were ever going to start taking care of your health, when do you think would be the best time to start?"

The subordinate question is so significant. Many times, I've had people ask of me when and where can you learn how to ask those questions. Well, in most of our towns in America, at your better bookstore, you will find one of the finest training manuals for that available today. It's called the Holy Bible. It has nothing to do with religion at this moment, but if you will get that Bible, get a red-letter edition, which has the words of Jesus Christ in red.

Regardless of their beliefs or lack of beliefs, any fair-minded person has to admit that the carpenter from Galilee was the greatest salesman who ever lived, and easily the greatest sales manager who ever lived. He took twelve salesmen—and one of them was certainly a loser—and they spread the word all over the world.

A lot of times I've had people say, "I read the Bible, but I don't understand it." I don't think it's the part they don't understand that bothers them. Actually the Bible is very clear, isn't it?

So you learn how to ask questions. Why? Because every time somebody asked Jesus a question, he answered it either with a question or with a parable. Want to know how to ask questions? That's the place to learn. As long as you're in there, you might as well read the answer, because one of these days, he's going to ask you a question, and if you get it right, you get to stay.

Questions are very, very important, but I want to close with his. The professional salesperson, I mean the real professional, is wise in that he knows that his own sales and his own career are going to move along much faster if his fellow salespeople are doing well and if his company is doing well. In short, he becomes a team player.

I was intrigued with the fact that back in 1986, the national championship in football was won by Penn State when they played the University of Miami. Miami had a Heisman Trophy winner on that particular team—Vinny Testaverde. He was a remarkable athlete and football player, but the Penn State team won the game.

When Penn State played Boston College, Boston had the Heisman Trophy winner, Doug Flutie; Penn State won the game. When Penn State played the University of Southern California, USC's Marcus Allen was the Heisman Trophy winner; Penn State won the game. When Penn State played the University of Georgia, which had the Heisman winner Herschel Walker, Penn State won the game.

I'm not trying to take anything at all away from these four young men, who are outstanding individuals and remarkable athletes, but I am saying that regardless of how good we are, regardless of how talented we are, as individuals and professionals, when we get involved in the team spirit, we individually will be doing better because our team is doing better. I believe that's one of the most important secrets of successful selling.

CHAPTER 12

The Keys to Successful Selling, Part 2

Zig

In our last presentation, we looked at some ideas and some keys that will make a difference in your sales career. John Shedd, president of Marshall Field and Company, once said, "We don't need to be told, but we do need to be reminded." So let me share with you the first five keys we dealt with.

We dealt with the key of *positive projection*. We dealt at length with the key of the *assumptive attitude*. We dealt with *physical action*. Then, *enthusiasm*, and the last key we dealt with was the *subordinate question*.

Now we're going to look at six additional keys. The first key we're going to look at now is key number six, which is the *key of listen*. Listening is such an important skill. It's hard, if not impossible, to listen your way out of a sale. As a matter of fact, on everybody's list of desirable qualities, a good listener has to rate right there at the top.

It is important that we do learn how to listen, but there's a couple of things about it that I want to emphasize. One is when the prospect says no, we need not to hear that. Oftentimes we don't even want to hear it.

We also need to learn how to listen, not just with our ears, but also with our eyes. For example, the prospect is saying, "No, I wouldn't give you that much money for one of these automobiles," but all the time they're gently stroking the upholstery. Their mouth is saying, "Too much money, and I won't buy it," but their body is saying, "Look, friend, all you have to do is convince me. I'm interested. Make it worth the money to me, and then we'll go ahead and buy."

One prospect might say, "No, this home is just too far out of town." Then they walk to that back bedroom, where that big picture window is, and they look out at that gorgeous view. You need to be listening not only with your ears but also with your eyes, and as I said earlier, when the prospect says no, you definitely do not want to always hear that one.

I have a good friend, one of the most remarkable ladies I think I've ever met. Her name is Merley Hoke. Merley was from Great Falls, South Carolina. Merley had one of the most peculiar hearing problems I think I have ever experienced. A customer could get right down in her face and say, "No, Merley, I don't want to buy." Merley wouldn't bat an eyelash. She hadn't heard a thing. I've seen them whisper "Yes," at sixty paces, and Merley picked up every syllable.

An amazing lady. She was one of the most consistent people I've ever seen in the world of selling. She was professional. She had memorized her handling of objections. She had memorized her closes to the degree that they were so natural you never would have even remotely suspected that they were memorized.

I've watched her on sales calls a number of times, and this was one of the little phrases she always used. She would make it her business to be seated directly in front of the lady. As she would start her closing move, she would invariably pick up her chair and begin to move to the other side. She would reach up, and she would put her hand on the lady's shoulder. She always said exactly the same thing: "This is so beautiful, and you deserve to have it, and I'm going to 'hep' you"— that's H-E-P—"I'm going to 'hep' you get it."

You got the distinct feeling that it was Merley and this lady, and they were ganging up on that big, old cookware company up there, they have thousands of sets of cookware, and "Bless your heart, you haven't even got one. I'm going you to help you get it."

She always used the other person's money, but Merley was an assistant buyer. She had moved literally, figuratively, emotionally, and every other way to the prospect's side of the table. Learn to listen, but when the prospect says no, please understand that the reason they say N-O is that they do not K-N-O-W enough to say yes. They don't know enough of the benefits.

This is the most important key. The next is the most misunderstood key. It is the *key of persistence.* A lot of people think of the persistent salesman as that individual who sits on you. "You're going to get it sooner or later, sign here," or "You know you want it. All your neighbors are getting it, sign here."

That's not persistence. That is downright foolishness. Those are the kind of salespeople who are not exactly a credit to our profession.

I really did not understand what real persistence was until a number of years ago, when I was touring Australia with World Book Encyclopedia. I was working with the managing director, a man named John Nevin, and we were speaking in all of the more cities in Australia for World Book.

On the trips, John and I had a chance to do a lot of chatting. He shared with me a story which has a tremendous impact on John's career and has had a substantial impact on mine. He got started as a part-time salesperson, as many of us did when we first entered the world of selling.

Now this was a number of years ago, and in most instances this simply is no longer done, but John was on a sales call one evening. He called on this German couple. They'd only been in Australia about six months. Their command of the English language was very limited. They really looked more like grandparents than parents. The mother had given birth to their one and only son when she was forty-four years old. She was short and stocky. John started that sales presentation at 8:00. It was after midnight before the sale was closed. When it was, John had to have the lady along as he left the home, because there was a vicious dog, and she had to escort him. She got outside the gate and closed it. John's reasonably tall. She was very short.

The lady reached up, put her hands on John's shoulders, and said, "Tank you, tank you, young man, for staying until we know what these books do for our boy. Tank you, tank you." John said it gave him a completely new understanding of the importance of what he was doing.

Sometimes when we sell a product for a long period of time, we grow accustomed to it. We grow accustomed to living in a nice home and wearing nice clothes, driving a nice car, having our family covered with an adequate amount of life insurance. We grow accustomed to all those things, and sometimes we take it as routine when we're making a sales call.

John said, "You know, Zig, that opened my eyes so clearly, and I realized and promised myself that I would have that renewed commitment, that renewed enthusiasm, that renewed sense of urgency and that willingness to persist until either the sale had been closed or it was evident that they either would not buy or could not buy."

Talking with John gave me a new perspective on the word *persistence*. I believe there's a better word for it. The word is *belief.* If you believe in what you're selling, you will persist. You'll do it professionally. You'll do it politely. You will do it as courteously and graciously as you can, but the professional who fervently believes that the prospect benefits with ownership of what they're selling will persist.

Next is the *key of the impending event.* An impending event is anything that is going to happen in your industry or to your company or to your product which will have an impact or an influence on your prospects and on your customers.

For example, in our own company, for several months now we have been selling our clients on the concept that we have something new and exciting coming out. Get ready. I know you do the same thing when you have new products coming out.

When I was in the life-insurance business, when you get six months and one day past your last birthday, you are now a year older in a lot of the tables, and we used that as an impending event. Many of you are selling products or goods or services right now that will be higher in price a year from now than they are today.

As salespeople, we need to capitalize on that: "Mr. Prospect, if you buy today, if you invest today, then you will save this amount of money." That impending event really does make a significant sales tune. We need to be tuned in to the times if we're going to sell as much as we should be selling.

The next key is kind of unusual. It's what we call the *key of inducement.* I have a pair of cufflinks that I happen to believe are the most beautiful cufflinks in the whole world. I really do. That redheaded wife of mine gave me these cufflinks for our twenty-fifth wedding anniversary. They're in the shape of an arrow. The arrow is in fact my, or our, emblem, and it's pointing up, of course. See you at the top.

When I got these cufflinks—and the diamonds are not the biggest in town by any stretch of imagination, but they are very significant—I made myself a promise: "I'm not going to wear any shirt again unless it has French cuffs, so I can wear these cufflinks."

So I went looking for some French-cuff shirts. This was a number of years ago. I'd walk in a store, and I'd say, "Do you have any French-cuff shirts?"

They'd say, "No."

I went into a dozen different stores. "Do you have any French-cuff shirts?"

"No, I don't."

"Do you know where I can get them?"

"No, I don't. Besides, didn't you see I'm busy? I was talking to this other clerk here." That wasn't exactly what they said, but it was almost that bad.

I was speaking up in Burlington, Iowa for the Chamber of Commerce. At the Chamber of Commerce where I was speaking, there was a gentleman with a white suit of clothes on. I'll tell you I thought that was the sharpest-looking suit of clothes I'd ever seen. I said to myself, "Self, you have to get you a suit just like that." So I cornered the fellow and asked him where he got it.

"I got it over in Fort Madison," he said, "at Glasgow Clothiers. There's a fellow there named Doyle Hoyer."

"I think I'm going to scoot over there tomorrow morning and get me one just like it."

"I'm going over tomorrow morning," he said. "I'd be pleased to take you."

"That'd be wonderful," I said.

He took me over, introduced me to Doyle, and I asked, "Doyle, do you have this white suit?"

"What size do you wear?"

"I wear a 41. I can slip on—now it will vary depending on the cut of the suit—but in most cases, I can slip on a size 41, sometimes it's a 42, and all I have to do is cuff the trousers, and I can walk right out in it."

"Yes, I've got that size."

I slipped the suit on—perfect fit. He measured the trousers to cuff them. I said, "How long will it take me to get this suit, Doyle?"

"I thought you said you weren't leaving until 2:00," he said.

"I'm not."

"Man, you're going to take this suit of clothes with you." Then he turned to the young man standing there and said, "Take this suit of clothes up to the tailor, and tell him I want it right now."

Then he turned to me, smiled, and said, "Now, Zig, I have something I really want to show you."

I left there with two suits, three sport outfits, and five pair of slacks and all the good stuff that goes along with it. As we were concluding, something was said about shoes, and I said, "No, Doyle. I'm well pleased with my shoes. I don't really need any."

He didn't hear a thing I said. He said, "Man, you have to look at these," and right straight to the shoe department he went.

As it turned out, I didn't find any shoes that I really liked that day, and I was getting ready to leave, but as an afterthought I said, "Oh, by the way, Doyle, do you have any French-cuff shirts?"

"No, I haven't," he said, "but I can get them for you."

A couple of weeks later, I got a telephone call from Doyle. He said, "Zig, did you get your French-cuff shirts?"

"Yes, I did."

"How do you like them?"

"Doyle, I just love them." I'd only gotten a half-dozen shirts from him because I wanted to see what kind they were and how they looked and that sort of thing.

Let me emphasize a point here. At that point in my career, outside of Yazoo City, Mississippi and my next-door neighbor, there weren't an awful lot of people who knew who Zig Ziglar was. Fort Madison, Iowa was nearly a thousand miles away, but he's calling to find out if I got those shirts and if I liked those shirts.

About a month later, I was in Kansas City in the airport. I saw a young fellow with a suit of clothes on.

Just loved it. (You're going to find out how I choose some of my clothes here in a minute.) I walked over and asked him, "Do you mind sharing with me where you got that suit of clothes and what kind it is?"

"Of course," he said. "I'd be delighted to."

He let me see the label, and I wrote down the brand and the number and all that good stuff. I called old Doyle and said, "Doyle, do you have such-and-such a suit?"

He said, "No, I haven't—but I can get it for you."

A couple of weeks later, he called me and said, "Did you get your suit? I said, "I sure did."

"How do you like it, Zig?"

"Oh, I love it, Doyle. It's absolutely beautiful."

About a month later I called him again. He said, "Zig, are you still at (214) 233-9191?"

"Yes, I am," I said.

"I was just fixing to call you."

"Yes, and I know what you're going to tell me too."

"You do?"

"Sure. You're going to tell me that you just got in the most beautiful new shipment of suits you have ever had in your life. You're going to tell me that you're going to send a dozen of them down to me and you're going to let me pick out exactly what I want and send the rest of them back."

"Zig, you are a genius."

When I start talking about common-sense sales techniques, this is one of the things I'm talking about. I am not color-blind, but I am color-ignorant. I do not know what goes with anything. I really don't. So Doyle will send me the suit, send the shirt, send me the tie, pick out the socks, put it in a little package, and attach a little note: "Dear Zig, these go together."

What is the key of inducement? There's a chance that Doyle Hoyer is saving me money. He declares on his Scout's honor that he is, and he might well be. Let me tell you what Doyle Hoyer really is saving me. It's time.

I spend less than an hour a year choosing my clothes, because he'll send me the clothes, I will take them down to the tailor close to my barbershop, where I have to go anyhow, and I time the trips together. It only takes a matter of minutes for me to get them. This relationship is a most unusual one.

I never will forget about five years ago, he called me to tell me about this tremendous new sports coat he had. As he started to describe it, I said, "Doyle, how much does that coat cost?"

"Zig, don't worry about it," he said. "I'm going to treat you right."

I don't know why I bothered to ask. He never tells me the price anymore, because he knows that over the years, he has developed a relationship of absolute trust based on his own integrity. He simply sends me the clothes. If I like them, I keep them and pay for them, and if I don't like them, I send them back.

Why am I devoting such a tremendous amount of time to this one simple example? I think it says an awful lot. In the intervening years—neither of us have any idea of the amount, but I've an idea that Doyle Hoyer's business has reaped at least a half-million dollars in sales, maybe as much as a million dollars, over all of these years.

Obviously I haven't bought that much clothing, but Doyle tells me that as a result of this conversation in my book and in my audio presentations and seminars, people call him every day and say, "If you'll treat me like you treat old Zig, we're going to do some business together."

What's my major point? There's no such things as a little sale. No such thing as a little sale. There are sales that grow. You know the story. From the mighty oak we started with an acorn. From a little sale, a lot of times you build a tremendous amount of business.

What's the inducement? I believe it's the greatest inducement of all. It is the personal interest and integrity of the salesperson who believes that he's going to benefit by serving the needs of his prospects. It's part of the concept: you can have everything in life you want if you'll just help enough other people get what they want.

The next key is one which I might say is the most important one. It's the *key of sincerity*. I've had many salespeople say to me, "I called on this account, and they'd been called on a dozen different times, and as they were buying they would say, 'You know, I don't really know why I'm giving you the business. I turned down three other people.'" Then they would give the reason: "But you seemed so sincere in what you were saying."

See, selling is a transference of feeling. When you can make your prospect feel about your product like you feel about your product, if it's humanly possible, they're going to end up buying your product. Selling is that transference of feeling.

Don't hang your hat too much just on being sincere, because if you sincerely believe in what you're doing, and if you're sincerely interested in your prospect's best interest, you're going to learn as much as you can as a professional to use the right procedures and the right techniques to help them own something that's going to benefit them.

One of the greatest stories I have ever heard is the story of Charles Laughton. He was a British Shakespearean actor. Charles Laughton toured our country reading the Bible. I never had the privilege of hearing him do that, but they say that he read the Bible in an incredibly beautiful, magnificent way, and brought those words to life.

He was reading in a large, rural church in a Midwestern community. When he finished, an awe, a hush fell over the audience. Some said it lasted two or three minutes. Then a little old man, he must have been about seventy-five years old, stood up and asked for permission to read the Bible.

It was granted, and as he started to read, it was obvious instantly to everyone there, including the great Charles Laughton, that this man had a limited education, that he did not have the diction or the elocution, and he mispronounced some of the words. But it was even more obvious to everyone there, and especially to Charles Laughton, that if this had been a Bible reading contest, Charles Laughton would have in fact finished a very distant second.

When it was all over, somebody came to the great English actor and asked, "How do you feel?"

Laughton, with a rather wry smile, said, "Well, I knew the script, and I knew it well, but this old man knew the author."

You can learn your presentation. You can learn every word, every dialogue. You can learn every facet of demonstrating your product, and if you're a professional, that's what you're going to do. But, my friend, a lot of people still miss success by about ten inches, because that's the distance from the head to the heart.

A high jumper broke a world's record. Somebody said, "How did you do it?"

He said, "I threw my heart over the bar, and the rest of me followed."

When you communicate the information you have in your head with the feeling you have in your heart, you will persuade more people to take action. What am I saying? That the salesperson is the most important part of the sales process.

The eleventh key that I want to share with you has to do with the *narrative story* or *narrative event*. It really is an effective way to help you remember the keys that we've been talking about.

A number of years ago, we were living in Columbia, South Carolina. On a Saturday morning, I walked into the den and said to my son, who was four years old, "Son, would you like to go to the grocery store?" He said, "Sure, Daddy," and he hopped up, and he put on his little boots, and we hopped in the car and drove down to the grocery store.

As we walked in the store, I got the basket and turned to the right to start getting the food. My son had seen a display of rubber balls straight ahead. He made a beeline for it. He got one of those balls, ran back over, popped that ball right in the basket, and stood there grinning from ear to ear.

I've never talked to my son at any length about this, but I've an idea that when I said to him, "Son, would you like to go to the grocery store?" the reason he said, "Sure, Dad," was that in that little active four-year-old mind, he was already thinking, "If I get my Daddy down at that store, I'm going to get me something. Don't know what it is, but I'm going to get me something."

He was already using the *key of positive projection*. The instant we walked in, he assumed that he'd better take some physical action, which he did with a considerable amount of enthusiasm. That boy used four keys on me in about four seconds flat.

I reached into the basket, I took that ball out, and I said, "Son, you already have a dozen balls. You don't need another one," and I handed it to him. "Now take it back."

My boy looked up at me and said, "Daddy, can I just hold the ball?"

What would you have done? The boy is only four years old. He doesn't want to buy the ball. He's only asked me a very simple subordinate question. What kind of daddy would I have been to say, "No, boy, you can't even hold the ball. Now take it back"? I wasn't about to do that, so I said, "OK, son. You can hold it a few minutes, but don't get any ideas. You are not going to buy that ball."

He didn't want to buy it. He just wanted to hold it. We walked around a few minutes, and we went past the display of rubber balls. I reached into my son's arms, took the ball out, put it back in the display, and said, "Son, you've held it long enough. You're going to fool around, drop it, get it dirty, and then Dad will have to buy it, and you just don't need another ball."

With that, I turned and walked away. Well, my boy was not listening when I said no, because he went right back to the display, snatched that ball back out, ran back to the basket, popped it right back in, and again stood there grinning.

You have to confess that he was one persistent little salesman. I'm kind of persistent myself, so I reached back into the basket, took it out, and as I headed for the display saying, "Son, I've told you for the last time now, you cannot have this ball," and when I started to walk back to the display, I looked down and there he stood, all thirty-nine pounds of him.

At that time, he talked with a slight lisp. He looked up at me, and he said, "Daddy, I wish you'd buy me that ball. I'll give you a 'tiss." That was an impending event, I'll tell you.

You talk about an inducement. What else could a four-year-old boy give his daddy? Sincere—in my lifetime, I have never dealt with a more sincere salesperson before or since.

Anyhow, for a long time thereafter, in the Ziglar household, we had thirteen rubber balls. I also must share this with you.

I've said I've never seen where a woman had given birth to a salesperson. That's not quite true because on February 1, 1965, in Columbia, South Carolina, the local paper carried a small headline: "Birth of a Salesman Announced. Mr. and Mrs. Zig Ziglar announced the birth of a salesman, John Thomas Ziglar, born February 1, 9:04 p.m., Providence Hospital, Columbia, South Carolina."

Now don't you misunderstand. I am not trying to influence my boy's career. He can sell anything he wants to. That's up to him.

If you'll buy these ideas and use these keys, you too can sell more of what you're selling, and you will have a more successful career.

13

CHAPTER

Professional Closing Techniques

Zig

According to sales trainer Chris Haggerty, 63 percent of all sales interviews end with no attempt to close. As a sales trainer, I can tell you that I've been on many a sales call where the salesperson talked and talked and talked, and finally the prospect would say, "Well, John, you're not trying to sell me something, are you?" The salesperson would just throw up his hands, "Oh, no, no, no."

Well, what are you? A professional visitor? As I understand it, the purpose of the call is to sell. Closing actually is an attitude. Closing is not pressure selling. Closing, however, is where we often are introduced to what we call the colorful salesman, simply meaning he's yellow.

I love what my good friend Fred Smith says. A lot of times, some of our prospects are not quite as gentle with us as we wish they were. That's another way of saying sometimes, not often, but sometimes, they're downright ornery. They're even rude and ugly. But Fred says when that happens, they're not rude and ugly because they want to hurt you, but because in most cases they are hurting. Now, my friend, if you can understand and accept that, I can assure you that your attitude will be a lot better, and your results will be a lot better in the world of selling.

I love what Frank Bettger said a number of years ago: "When you forget yourself and remember what the other person gets out of the sale, all of your energy will be concentrated on the other person and their benefits." When you're handling it that way, in no way could you ever be accused of being manipulative or high-pressure. As a matter of fact, you will be practicing the philosophy we talk about so much: that you can have everything in life you want if you'll just help enough other people get what they want.

Many years ago, or so the story goes, a fox and a rabbit were having a cool one in the local pub. The fox was doing a considerable amount of talking. He was bragging. He said, "You know, I have so many ways to get away from the hounds if any of them should come. I could either scoot up in the attic real quick, or I could hop out of here, and go down to the creek, and lose them in the water, or I could, for that matter, double-track and backtrack several times. I could lose them a dozen different ways, or go up a tree. There's no way they'd ever get me."

The rabbit said, "I'm afraid I can't do all of those things. If the hound should come, all I can do is just run like a scared rabbit." About that time, the baying of the hounds were heard close by. The fox said, "What should I do? Do I go up in the attic, or do I run out here and get in the stream and confuse them that way? Or should I get out there and backtrack a few times or climb up a tree?"

While he was mediating on the subject, the hounds came and ate him. Of course, the rabbit didn't know all of those things. The minute he heard the hounds, he just ran like a scared rabbit.

What am I saying with that? I'm saying that it is better to know one or two or three good closes and use them professionally, than to know fifty closes and not use any of them.

But don't you take too much comfort in what I just said. The real professional will learn a number of closes so well that they become an innate, subliminal, instinctive part of his repertoire so that he can use them at the time they're needed.

You see, closing is an attitude, and believers are closers.

What do I mean by that? Several years ago I spoke for one of the major life insurance companies out on the West Coast. It was their national convention. They had their top people from all over the country along with their wives. There were about 2000 of them. I was having breakfast with the president, and we got to talking.

He explained to me that he could take any 100 of his salespeople, and provided they had been selling for at least one year, he could, without checking a single sales record, tell you within five percentage points what the entire group would produce for the year. He said, "You know, Zig, all I'd have to do is look at the amount of life insurance they carried on their own life, and then I could predict within five points what they were going to sell, because the depth of their belief in the product will determine their success in the sale of the product."

If you're selling Ford automobiles, you ought to be driving a Ford. If you're selling Chevys, you ought to be driving a Chevy. When you believe in your product, you will be using that product. Now I don't necessarily believe that if you sell 747s, you have to buy one, but I do believe that within reason, your belief ought to include yourself and your family.

The professional closer builds a closing consciousness just as a football player has a scoring consciousness, particularly when they get down close to the end zone. In the NFL, the last two minutes of the first half, and the last two minutes of the game, they will score 30 percent of their total scores, because they have drilled and planned. They have gotten that instinct up, and the game plan is there. So they score much more.

A lot of times I've heard a coach say, "We had them on the ropes, but we just didn't put them away." A lot of times we get within sight of the sale, and then we just don't ask for the order. We don't close.

Now let's look at some closes or techniques which will produce some business and produce it at the time you really need it—or want it, I should say—and in most cases, that's going to be right now.

A lot of times a prospect will say to you, "Your product costs too much." A simple question will be helpful: "Mr. Prospect, wouldn't you agree that it's hard to pay too much for something you really want?"

It's amazing, but if you're selling a low-ticket item, a lot of times that really sets them to thinking, and they often will say, "You know, I never thought about it that way, and I really do like it." If you're selling an expensive item, all that will do will get their mind to function and thinking in the right direction. A lot of times, that's the first step towards the close. A lot of times, though, they will still come back and say, "It costs too much."

Then we respond with a question. "Wouldn't you agree, Mr. Prospect, that it's better to invest more than you planned instead of less than you should? If you invest more than you planned, you're talking about pennies. If you invest less than you should, and it won't do the job, then you've wasted it all."

Let me get you ladies to answer a couple of questions, and see if we can establish what I mean. Do you have some cosmetics in the drawer at home that have been there for several months that you're not using and you definitely know you're never going to use? You're not going to throw them away, because they're still good, and it'd certainly be wasteful to throw them away, so you'll wait another year or two, when they're dried out and have no value at all. Then you can throw them away with a clear conscience.

Here's my question, ladies. Wouldn't it have been better to have invested a little more than you had planned instead of a little less than you did? You see, you've lost a whole package now. If you had invested a little bit more, it would have been pennies.

I'm not just talking about the ladies. Guess what Old Zig did one day before I lost this weight. I went to a suit sale. A beautiful $350 suit. This was some while back, and they had it on sale for $175. Now, it was not my size, but I was going to lose that weight. Half price on a deal like that—you bet you I bought it. Wore it one miserable time before the moths got to it. A hundred and seventy-five dollars to wear a suit one time! That's an exorbitant price.

Yes, it is better to invest a little more than you had planned instead of a little less than you should. One way you're talking about pennies; the other way you're talking about real dollars.

The prospect might say, "it still costs too much."

"Mr. Prospect, let me ask you this. Are you talking about price or cost?" A lot of times, a prospect is confused on that. Most of the time, they come back and say, "What do you mean, am I talking about price or cost?"

Let me share with you an example. It's out of my own life. It happened to me, it's legitimate, it's real, but it's important for you to understand that you're going to have to take this example and make it applicable to your own situation.

When my son was six years old, we went down to get him a bicycle. This was sixteen years ago, so things have changed since then, but we went to the Schwinn bicycle shop, and the price of the bicycle was $64.95. At that time, $65 for a bicycle for a six-year-old who's just going to tear it up anyhow was foolish.

So we went down to the economy bicycle shop, and we found a really neat little bicycle for just $34.95. That price was considerably less. We bought this one.

A couple of months later, when we went down to get the new handlebars, fortunately the bicycle was still under warranty, and it didn't cost us anything. A month or two later, though, we went back to get some more new handlebars, and this time, we had to dig up $4.50 more. About six weeks later, the sprocket apparatus came completely unzipped. By the time they got through with that, it was $15 and change.

About a month later, the bearings in the front wheel came unzipped, and we went down again. This time they said $3, $4, $5, or $6. I've forgotten what it was, because I threw in the towel. I said, "No way." At that point, we had invested $54.45 in that little bicycle. My son actually rode that bicycle about

The Secrets of Successful Selling Habits

of that bicycle was $9 per month.

We went down and bought the Schwinn bicycle.

My son actively rode that Schwinn bicycle for about five years. He played riding it an additional five years. By that I mean, he made a dirt bike out of it, and he and a couple of his buddies, big old boys, much too big for it, had a ball on that little bicycle. He had it for ten years.

The only additional expenses involved were for a couple of tires, which had nothing to do with the quality of the bicycle. After ten years, when you put your pencil to it, this bicycle cost us $6.50 per year. The price of the first bicycle was $34.95 initially. Its cost was $9 a month. The price of this bicycle was $64.95. Its cost was $6.50 a year.

You look at your prospect and you simply say, "Now, Mr. Prospect, you know price is a one-time thing. Cost is a lifetime thing as far as a product is concerned. A lot of people can beat us on price, but nobody can beat us on cost." Obviously you want to make certain that statement is true. "Now I know you're most concerned with cost, aren't you?" Then it's simply a matter of working out the details. "When would you like to start saving this money? Shall we put this on this program or this plan?"

Closing can be, should be, and often is simply a routine, follow-through procedure. Here's one which is used more in the direct sales world and in real estate and several other areas, but because of changes in marketing strategies, it's being used more and more in a lot of different ways.

When I started my sales career, this one was known as the *granddaddy close*; that's the way they taught me. Other people called it the *basic close*; some call it the *order-book close*. About fifteen years ago, I met a young sales trainer named Gene Montrose up in Portland, Oregon, who identified this as the *disclosure close*. I believe that's the best I've ever heard, and since then I've been using that.

Here's the scene. You've demonstrated the product, the goods, or the services. At this point you need to communicate to the prospect exactly what the terms are. A lot of people don't buy because they don't really understand what the offer is. That sounds strange, but a lot of times, they really don't understand whether it's twelve payments at $18 or eighteen payments at $12. They don't understand what they get with this particular price breakdown and what they get with the other one. So when I talk about disclosure, I'm really talking about clarification.

You lead into it, and it works like this. You have your materials out, your order book is there, and you say, "You know, Mr. or Mrs. Prospect, Uncle Sam enters our lives in a lot of different ways. One thing they did a few years ago, which we think is excellent, is they started requiring that all companies in this industry reveal the exact terms of the transaction, all of the hidden charges, to each customer. Legitimate companies are delighted to do that. Our company decided to take it one step further. Instead of just revealing to our customers all of the terms, they now require us to reveal to every single person we talk with exactly, written out in black and white, what the offer is."

You've just laid the stage for writing the order. On the playback of this, you'll really pick up on that. Then you say to your prospect, "For example, the serial number or product number we've been talking about is order number 98," and you just write *number 98.* "The retail value of this is $399.95." It's not major, but I leave the dollar mark off on purpose. "The shipping and handling on this particular order is $20, and that brings it to $419.95. Uncle Sam steps into the picture along with the state, and they extract an additional $30, so the total price is $449.95." If you'll notice, I have not put their name on this.

Many times along about now, the prospect will say to you, "Wait a minute, I didn't say I was going to buy anything." Then you can honestly and legitimately look at the prospect and say, "Of course, you didn't. As a matter of fact, Mr. Prospect, I don't believe anybody, you or me either, would ever decide to buy or not to buy something until they had enough of the information or facts to make the decision. All I'm doing is giving you the exact offer."

Many times they say, "OK."

Then I would say, "Let me ask you question. *If*"—I use this word extremely hard—"*if* you were to go ahead with this, would it be more convenient to handle it on our $20 each month deposit program, or would you prefer the sixty-day cash plan?" You've just closed there on an alternate of choice. A lot of times they repeat it back: "*If*, now I did say *if*, I were to go ahead and get it, I'd have to handle it at the $20 deposit each month."

Then we move into another alternate of choice, which really involves a minor decision, and a lot of times a minor decision will carry the major decision. "One thing I should mention, Mr. Prospect, is with this particular order, you have a couple of options. You can, for example, choose this electric keyboard to go with it, or it might be that you would prefer this entire set of cassettes to reinforce it."

You could also offer a different item, like a knife sharpener or a cleaning brush. It doesn't have to be anything at all other than something of another nature, like for example, "I neglected to mention this comes in two-tone brown and solid gray. Which *would*—" and the strong word in this case is *would*— "which *would* you prefer?"

If they say, "I suppose I would like this particular option," then you simply take them one more step, and the word is *in*. "*In* getting this, would it make any difference whether the deposits fell on the first or the fifteenth, or would the twenty-fifth be better?"

Then they say, "It doesn't really matter. Why don't you put them on the twenty-fifth?" Now you obviously say, "This is Mr. and Mrs. J.J. Johnston, isn't it?"

People say, "Ziglar, does that kind of stuff work?" I say, "No, not all the time," but a good close is not going to make anybody buy anything they don't want. But this particular thing clarifies what the offer is. On many occasions, I covered this, and then twenty minutes later, the prospect, having thought about it as we go through some other things, would say, "How long did you say those payments would be, and when would the first one be?"

They have gone back to their thought process, and so you still are in the sales ball game. This one reveals the information. Yes, the disclosure close is a very significant one. You've established something that includes that alternate of choice on two different occasions. That's the minor decision we're talking about.

Elmer Wheeler, one of the early great sales trainers in our country, used that one effectively. You might have heard the story. Back during the Depression, he was commissioned by the Walgreen Drug Company to see what he could do about building their counter business at the soda fountain. In those days, they sold an awful lot of malted milks. Eggs during the Depression were between 10 and 15 cents a dozen, but when they included an egg in a malted milk, they got an extra nickel for it, so you can see what impact that would have on the bottom line.

Elmer came up with one little thing. When somebody would come in and ordered a malted milk or a milkshake, the clerks were trained to pick up two eggs and say, "Did you want one egg or two with this milkshake?" The customer had not thought of an egg at all, but thinking that one was less than the two, they would often say, "One's enough." They sold hundreds of extra cases of eggs every week as a result of that.

The question often comes up, "When do you try to close?" You close early, you close often, and you close late, but don't ever forget this: you never close, or attempt to close, until you've established value. A lot of times, little things make a big difference in whether or not we're going to make a sale. Sometimes a sale is not selling somebody a product, goods, or services, but the sale is selling somebody on the idea of letting us represent them or giving us that job.

Hockfield & Associates, which is a manufacturers' rep firm just outside of Chicago, recently got a major line to sell because of the way they answered the telephone. That's right. They answered the telephone like we do: "Good morning, it's a great day." There were several other firms that were in competition. Everything else seemed to be equal, and the president of the company said, "This is what made the difference with us." A little incidental thing can make the difference.

Several years ago, I was calling on a firm to sell them sales training. The size of the order that I was seeking was $18,000. That was the proposal. There were four guys involved, and they were very compatible. They were enthused about what we were doing, and they definitely were interested in buying. They said, "We're going to talk it over, and weigh it and evaluate, and then we'll get in touch with you."

I smiled and said, "In other words, just as soon as you get around to it, you'll be back to me."

They said, "Yes, we will. You can absolutely count on it. When we get around to it, we're definitely going to buy."

My business card is a little unusual. It's round, and on one side it has my name and address. On the other side it has a word. It's T-U-I-T. I pulled four of these out. I handed it to the four guys and said to them, "Well, gentlemen, I know that you're men of integrity, and when you say you're going to do something as soon as you get around to it, I know you're going to do it. So here's your 'round tuit.'"

They laughed uproariously and gave me the order. You might say, "Ziglar, you have to be kidding me. You mean they bought because you used a round tuit? No, that's not the reason they bought. The reason they bought is they were sold on what we were doing, and they fully intended to buy. This was a humorous way to move them over into the purchase column. As I say, it is oftentimes a little thing that will make a difference in whether you get it or don't get it.

Good closing is not always recognized even by those who are experts in the field. We built a home back in 1983 down at Holly Lake, which is 120 miles east of where we live in Dallas. That's where we go to do our writing.

We were excited about that home, and Bill Tennyson was our builder. His wife is a famous interior designer. Her name is Joyce Winn, and she was most helpful. She was kind of thrown in the deal there if Bill built the house.

I shall never forget that day that we were there. We have a great room there. It's beautiful. It's thirty feet high. With a thirty-foot ceiling, you know you have a lot of wall space. One day we were down at the lake, and Bill and Joyce came by, and Joyce just happened to have a beautiful wall rug with her.

"You know, Zig," she said, "I've been thinking about this. You all have this big, empty wall there, and I believe that this would really enhance the appearance." You probably already suspect that since she decorates for beautiful hotels all over this country, this wasn't exactly dime-store merchandise that she was presenting. When she told us what the investment would be, I didn't exactly jump up and down and say, "Whoopee." I said, "I don't know about that, Joyce."

"Well, Bill's with me," she said, "and I'll tell you what let's do. We'll just go ahead and hang it, and it might fit, or it might not fit, but you let it hang there a couple of days, and then you'll know."

I said, "That's fine. That makes sense to me." They put the wall rug up.

Three hours later, in my jog, all of the sudden it hit me what she had done to me. One of the oldest of the old. That's right. She had used that old puppy-dog close on me, and I don't need to tell you this, but we still have that wall rug hanging there.

The most important factor as a closer is the integrity of the salesperson. This might shock you a little when I say this, but many times you'll sell more by not selling at all. Although I said "many times," in reality I don't believe it will be many times. But I do believe there are those occasions when your integrity will be such that you won't make the sale.

Let me give you a specific example. Several years ago at Christmas, we went down to get my son a bicycle. We walked into the Schwinn bicycle shop. Now I don't speak bicycle. It's a weird language. When I was a boy, we used to have wheels and spokes and handlebars and seats and brakes and that kind of stuff. Now it's weird what stuff they have on it and what they call it.

We walked in, and the owner of the store was talking to a grandmother who had her grandson with her. She didn't speak bicycle either, so she had an exact list. "This is the bicycle I want. The little boy across the street has this one. I'm going to get it for my grandson. Do you have this bicycle?"

The owner looked at it and said, "Yes. We have this exact bicycle, but ma'am, you're grandson is too small for this bicycle. He needs one smaller than that. He can't reach the pedals."

She said, "Oh, no, I want the best you have. I want one just like the little boy's across the street."

The owner said, "Ma'am, this is exactly like it. Same quality, same price, same everything, but it's a smaller size."

"Absolutely not. I have to have exactly what the little boy across the street has."

The owner said, "Ma'am, that bicycle would be dangerous. Your grandson cannot touch the pedals. If he should get out in the street, he would possibly lose control. There could be a tragic accident."

"I want what I want, or I won't get anything at all."

The owner looked at her and said, "Ma'am, this is probably going to shock you, but I cannot sell you that bicycle. I could not sleep at night knowing that there was a chance that your grandson would lose control of this someday and maybe get injured. I can't sell you the bicycle."

Incredibly enough, the grandmother turned around and walked away in an absolute huff.

You might say, "Ziglar, do you take your integrity that far?" You bet you. You take your integrity that far.

Since then, we've had occasion to buy a couple more items in that bicycle shop. I would send my son or my granddaughters in there to this day with a signed check, amount left open, made out to that store, and say to them, "You buy from him. I know he will do exactly what is right." That's the way you build a career.

Professional salespeople see themselves in that light, and they also see themselves as closers. I'm reminded of a story from the Vietnam War. There was a major in the Hanoi Hilton. His name was Major Nesmith, and he was in there about six or seven years. He was an avid golfer, not the best one in town. He played about a ten handicap, but he loved to play. During those years of confinement, he played golf in his mind: eighteen holes every single day.

As he played this golf, he played it in its entirety. He visualized himself on the tee box. He visualized himself hitting the ball. He visualized and in his mind took exactly the same number of steps. He played golf a solid five hours every day, visualizing everything. When he was released, the first time back on the golf course, without having held a golf club in his hand for nearly seven years, he shot par golf. He had seen it all the way.

The professional salesperson sees themselves. They visualize exactly what they're going to do. They practice, they learn, they study. The professional salesman is an incurable optimist. He's the kind of guy who'd put a dime in the shopping meter while his wife goes shopping.

When I think of that, I think of my friend Tom Fountain, who ran a service station a number of years ago in Decatur, Georgia. I'll never forget the day I met Tom. I pulled in, and it was raining cats and dogs. I coasted in.

As I pulled in, I hopped out of the car, I ran in, and I waved at him. "Don't fill the tank now. Wait until it lets off a little bit."

I walked in and said, "Man, this rain is really something, isn't it?"

Old Tom said, "Yes, it's absolutely beautiful."

"Tom," I said, "you're the first service-station operator I've ever seen in my life that said it was beautiful to see rain. Why would you say a thing like that?"

"Ah, Zig," he said, "at the moment, my gasoline business is down, but when we get a gully washer like this, you can't believe the nails and the glass and all of the sharp objects that's going to be washing out of driveways and yards out into the streets. We're going to have more tire-repair work in the next week than we've had in the last three months. Ah, it is beautiful, Zig." That's the professional salesperson attitude, you see.

Another one Tom taught me is this. This was in the days when service stations were service stations; they would check the oil and the gas, and they'd always check the fan belt. When he found a faulty one, he'd always say to the owner, "You have a bad fan belt. You could be stranded out on the road at any time. If you would get your spare out of the trunk, I'll put it on. It won't take me but a minute."

You know the rest of that story, don't you? "I don't have a spare back there." Tom said, "Well, you really need a fan belt."

The customer would say, "OK, let's put one on."

You know the rest of it, don't you? You know he came out with two fan belts.

Old Tom told me, "Zig, about one time out of five, I sold an extra fan belt. I'll never know how many people I kept from getting stranded in some small town late at night, but I feel good knowing that I probably did a lot of that."

The last little example on selling. As you've heard me say, I believe closing is important. For example, you're unemployed. You're looking for a job, or you are a youngster looking for your first job. Or your company has closed down. You'd been occupied in one field, and now you're in another one.

You're applying for the job, and they ask that old, familiar question: "What is your experience?" If you say, "I've been in engineering all of my life. I haven't had any experience in this department," your chances of getting that job are greatly diminished.

But you can honestly look at that individual and say, "Sir, I've had twenty-two years' experience in being on time every day for my job. I've twenty-two years' experience of giving honest effort every time I show up, twenty-two years' experience telling the truth, twenty-two years' experience in knowing that my job depends on the profitability of your company. I have learned to work in such a way that it will ensure your profitability, not because I'm such a good guy, but because I want the security of the job. I've had twenty-two years' experience in getting along well with those I work with and twenty-two years' experience of having a winning attitude.

"As for technical expertise, I've had twenty-two years' experience in learning, and I'm a good student. Sir, I believe that's the kind of experience you need in your company. I can start immediately, or would next week work into your plans better?"

Yes, I believe everything is selling, and I believe that with the right words, the right voice inflection, and above all being the right person, you can close more sales.

14
CHAPTER

Emotion versus Logic in Selling

Zig

According to my good friend and fellow sales trainer Merrill Frazier, in the next twenty-four hours, your prospect's heart will beat 103,689 times. His blood will travel 168,000 miles. His lungs will inhale 23,240 times. He'll eat three and a half pounds of food. He'll exercise only 7 million of his 9 billion brain cells. He'll speak 4800 words, of which 3200 involve something about himself, and not a single one will be about you, your products, or services unless you figure out a way to involve him emotionally with your sales situation.

The only way you're going to get your share of his attention and his words is to use your sales skill and the imagination to make yourself a part of his world.

In selling, preparation is often the key. In my early days as a speaker, I had a mentor named Dr. Emol Fails, at that time a professor at North Carolina State

University. Dr. Fails was conducting sales training seminars for the various Chambers of Commerce, particularly in the North Carolina area.

I vividly remember one of the ways he prepared for a sales call. He would take his wallet, tie a string around it, and attach it to the back bumper of his car. He would ride that wallet around town for several days until it absolutely was at the point of collapse. Then he would put his credit cards, his driver's license, and his money in it, and he would have to almost tie a string around it in order to keep it together.

When he would go into a town to sell a Chamber of Commerce on sponsoring the seminar, which was a three-evening training seminar for retail merchants, he would always go in to three or four local stores before he went to see the Chamber. He would go in and buy a necktie or a belt or some item that was right there at the counter where they sell wallets.

He'd get ready to pay, and in every case, he would drop that wallet. The sight was something to see. Credit cards, driver's license, money, and billfold would scatter all of the place. The people were always nice. The clerks would invariably get down on the floor and help him pick up the scattered things, but interestingly, not a one, not one ever, suggested that in addition to the necktie or the belt, maybe, just maybe, Dr. Fails would be in the market for a new wallet.

We often run right by sales situations because we're not prepared. I know you heard the story of the woodcutter whose production kept going down because he didn't have time to sharpen his ax. Abraham Lincoln put it this way: "If I had to cut a cord of wood and only had eight hours to do it, I'd spend the first three hours sharpening my ax."

A lot of times, preparation is entirely in the mind. In 1986, my good friend Jay Messenger, from down in Houston, Texas, who sells executive aircraft, sold one to Bob Hope. It is big, it is a $2 million deal, and obviously he took a picture of this transaction. Wouldn't you have done the same thing?

When he took this picture, he showed it to a friend, who said, "When did you make the sale?"

Jay said, "Four months ago."

The guy said, "I know better than that. Just last week you made that sale."

"No, it was four months ago," Jay said. "Four months ago, when I conceived the idea of selling this to Bob Hope, that's when I made the sale. Not selling was not an option. It was not an alternative. I planned it carefully. I visualized it. I took all of the steps, and missing the sale just simply was not an option."

That's professional selling. Jay's been selling very successfully for twelve years, but with the application of some of these principles, his success has moved forward at a much faster rate. Sometimes imagination is the key in closing the sale.

When I was in the insurance business, this one came out, and I used it, obviously because it worked. You know, according to the psychologists, we have a tendency to repeat pleasurable experiences. Since making a sale is a pleasurable experience, I used it dozens of times after that.

One evening I was not really making any progress on a presentation. I'd covered the standard objections. I'd answered his questions. The man could give me no legitimate reason for not buying it, yet I was no closer to the sale than I had been when I walked in the door.

In desperation, I reached up and grabbed this one. I said, "Mr. Prospect, perhaps I have been showing you the wrong program. Maybe what you need is our new twenty-nine-day agreement.

"Let me explain this agreement. It gives you the same, identical face amount of insurance. The retirement benefits are exactly the same, and you have been very clear that these are your first two considerations: first for the protection of the family, and second for your later use yourself. You also get a waiver of premium with this one, and you also get the double indemnity in the event the death is accidental. One of the beautiful things about this twenty-nine-day agreement is the fact that your monthly investment is only 50 percent as much as it is on the other agreement. Would that suit your needs better?"

The man grinned and said, "Well, it sure fits my pocketbook better, but what is this twenty-nine-day bit?"

"It means that you're covered twenty-nine days out of every month, and the company will let you choose the two days, or the one day, you do not wish to be covered. You might want to choose a weekend."

Then I said, "No, really, you'd probably be at home on the weekend, and that's the most dangerous place of all." I had to work at not laughing when I was doing this.

Then, I'd get real serious, and I'd say, "You know, Mr. Prospect, in all reality and fairness, if you were to run me out of here at this moment, I could understand because I'm making light of something which is very, very serious, and that is the protection and security of your family. To put your mind at ease, let me say this. There isn't an insurance commissioner in the world that would approve the sales of any such contract as that—no way. I know what you were thinking as I presented it to you. You were thinking to yourself, 'With my luck, something would happen to me on that one or two days each month that I'm not covered.' I simply used this method to alert you to the fact that if you would not leave your family unprotected one or two days out of the month, there is no way you are going to fail to protect your family the 365 days that are in the year.

"Now, Mr. Prospect, the beautiful thing about the program you and I have been talking about is that it covers you twenty-four hours a day, seven days out of the week, regardless of where you are and what you're doing. In reality, that's the kind of coverage you want for your family, isn't it?"

It's amazing what an impact that had. All I had done was to dramatize his situation, and a tremendous number of them responded in a very favorable way. You need to adapt that to your own situation.

This next one also is an insurance example, but as you'll see, it can easily be adapted to whatever business you're in. When I was in insurance, we did the two-part sales approach. We went in and got the interview, got the basic information, and did an appraisal on the family needs. Then our people would put the proposal together, and we'd go back for the presentation. There was a substantial amount involved. The final presentation generally took about forty-five minutes. Counting driving time and all, you have to figure on about two hours and a half for each call. So they were significant calls.

One thing that used to bug the life out of me—to tell you the truth it made me mad—was the fact that a lot of times after making a presentation, the prospect would say, "Mr. Ziglar, we obviously need the insurance. We recognize that, but I'm a little embarrassed that I permitted you to come back. You see, my wife's second cousin has a boyfriend whose neighbor's cousin has an uncle whose son is in college, and his roommate's best friend's brother is in the life-insurance business. If we bought, we'd have to buy from him."

Obviously it wasn't quite that bad, but it was bad enough that they knew, and I knew, and they knew that I knew that they weren't going to buy any insurance from anybody if they didn't do business with me. People are inclined along those lines. So I had to come up with something that would help me to overcome that objection, which I was getting pretty regularly. Then I thought of an idea as a result, incidentally, of reading Frank Bettger's book *How I Raised Myself from Failure to Success in Selling.*

I'd read that book ten years earlier. It is still a classic in the world of selling. It's one of the major reasons I spend so much time selling you on the idea of growing and learning and staying abreast. Anyway, I came up with an idea. The next time one of them hit me with that, I smiled all over. I couldn't wait. I almost planted the objection myself, as a matter of fact.

When they came up with that one, I said, "Well, Mr. Prospect, I'm confident that the individual you're speaking about is a fine person. I know if they're licensed in this state, they're OK. I know that if their company is licensed here, and obviously it is, that's fine. There's nothing at all wrong with either that individual, so far as I know, or with that company, but I can do something for you that no other insurance man alive can do for you."

"What's that?"

"Mr. Prospect, I can marry you," and with that I reached down, and I pulled from my briefcase a marriage certificate. It went something like this, beautifully done on parchment paper: "Certificate of Marriage. I, Zig Ziglar, on this eighteenth day of January, 1976," or whenever it was, "agree to the marriage between myself and John and Mary Smith." I'd already typed in their names in.

"By this agreement, Zig Ziglar agrees to stay abreast of all the trends in the industry as it relates to Social Security and other programs which directly relate to the lives and fortunes of John and Mary Smith. I agree to be available in time of need. John and Mary Smith agree to give Zig Ziglar the privilege of earning the right to serve."

Then I would say, "Now all it needs, Mr. and Mrs. Prospect, is your OK right here, and the marriage will be official." The response to it was absolutely amazing, mostly hilarious. They'd always laugh, and say—old boys especially would—"Ziglar, now is this a legitimate marriage? I mean, you're not going to get me involved with the law. This is not going to be bigamy or anything like that, is it?"

I'd laugh. I'd say, "No, I cleared it with the governor of the state. The insurance commissioner says it's fine. I've even gotten approval from my brother-in-law."

The prospect would just about always turn to his wife and say, "Honey, what do you think about it? Do you want to marry this fellow?"

She'd say, "Well, he wants to marry us both, and he looks like an all-right guy to me. Why don't we do it?"

The old boy would say, "Yes, let's go ahead," and he'd take his pen. Now you're talking about a signature. It'd be all over the page—laughing all the time.

But a funny thing happened on the way to the bank. I never once got the OK on the marriage agreement when I did not get the OK on the application for the insurance. See, it really was a trial close, wasn't it? A lot of people also like to do business with those who are just a little creative and a little different. Now you can get out in left field, and I'm not talking about that. I'm talking about within the bounds of good taste.

How do you use this in your particular industry? How can you translate it and make it work? One of our outstanding clients are Hockfield & Associates, the manufacturers' reps, just outside of Chicago—very successful.

Their salesperson had been calling on this particular company. His name is Wes Fenster, and Wes and Ed Hockfield got to debating on this particular one. It was a big account. They wanted the business, felt like they had a better program, a better product to offer, but the competition was just twenty-one miles away, right in the back door.

Wes stressed the quality of the product they were selling, stressed promptness and dependability of delivery, expressed the marketing ideas they had behind it, the reputation of the manufacturer, all of these things, but they were still making no progress.

Then one day Ed and Wes had a sales meeting. They said, "Which of this stuff that old Zig's been talking to us about can we use here?" They agreed that the marriage certificate would be the proper approach, and here's the way it came out:

"Certificate of Marriage terms of agreement: When you buy a private-label program from Hockfield & Associates and the Nice-Pak Company, you also buy me. I am literally going to be married to the Shopko account. I will see that you will receive the following: the finest products, the best possible service, the fairest price, to be kept on top of current trends, your personal representative, the highest quality, the best packaging," and right down the line.

Then, "By this certificate of marriage, Wes Fenster agrees to always be available for any event or need for service of any kind. Dennis Ruble and Shopko stores only agree to give Wes Fenster the privilege to serve."

The first year, that's approximately a half-million dollar account. Does imagination work? Does creativity work? Does really getting involved in what you're doing work? I say that it absolutely, emphatically, and positively does. Incidentally, the head honcho, the president of the company from whom they had taken the business, really got involved, and he went back to make the call to try to recapture the business, but it was no deal.

Imagination helps sometimes. More often, it will simply be an old standby that will produce the business. I'm going to tie two closes together here to show you what I mean: the tennis racket and the Ben Franklin. The first one you might not have heard of. The second one you undoubtedly have heard of, if you've been in selling very long at all.

Sometimes we're involved in a sales situation where you have two people who are going to be making the decision. It could be two partners. It could be husband and wife. They're tossing it back and forth, and one says, "What do you think?"

The other one says, "Well, it's up to you."

"No, you have to earn the money."

"Well, you're going to have to use it." Back and forth they go. They're batting that ball back and forth. What they're really saying is, "You decide."

"No, you decide."

"No, you decide."

That can mean one of two things. Both of them want to buy, but don't want to make the commitment, or neither one of them wants to buy or make the commitment. Or it could be the third one. One does and one doesn't, but neither one of them wants to say.

Now, particularly if it's between a husband and wife, and they bat it back more than twice, sure as shooting, one of them is then going to then knock it out of the ballpark, and it is generally the husband. He'll smile ever so pleasantly and say, "Well, I'm sure that we're going to end up getting it, but she can't make up her mind."

Bless his heart. How do you handle that? When the ball is passed across that net a couple of times, you hold up your hand and say, "'Scuse me." (In some parts of the country, they would say, "Excuse me," but that's wrong. It's "'Scuse me.") "I should not say this, perhaps, but I'm going to. I believe, Mr. and Mrs. Prospect, that neither one of you should make this decision. The reason is simply this. You're emotionally involved, and regardless of what you decide, if you decide yes, then later one of you might say, 'I tried to get you not to do that.' If you say no, the other one might say, 'If you'd have gone ahead and gotten that thing, we wouldn't be having this trouble.' When you're emotionally involved, it's not a good time to make a decision. Let me be so bold as to suggest that instead of letting emotion decide, why not let the actual facts make the decision?"

Now you've set it up for the Ben Franklin close. "Here's what I mean by letting the facts make the decision. Many years ago, one of the wisest men our country ever produced was a man named Benjamin Franklin. When Franklin was confronted with a decision which was very difficult, what he would do is take a sheet of paper and draw a line down the middle." Again, let me remind you that you need to be working on your pad at the same time. We are utilizing the prospect's sight—seeing is believing—and the sound of our voice; hearing is emotional. We're tying emotion and logic together.

"On one side Franklin would put *for*, and on the other side, he would write *against*, and he would go down the line listing the reasons *for*. That's what you want to do. For example, one reason you want to go ahead and make this move is that you really like the product. You like it, and you want it."

Let me tell you something. People are going to buy what they like and what they want. They'll figure out a way. You might have to come up with some creative financing for them, but they're going to work at buying what they like and what they want. Then you go right on down the list, and there should be a number of reasons for them to go ahead and buy.

Do not put numbers by them. That's important. The reason is this: you might get involved in a contest with your prospect. When they move to this side, they might say, "Now, you have seventeen or thirteen. Let me see if I can come up with more." They come up with some of the most asinine things you can possibly imagine.

You go down the list with some reasons you definitely should not make this move. Now I feel very strongly about this particular point: you need to list the one or two things that have been dominating the conversation.

If the prospect, for example, has been protesting, "We just don't have any money," you need to write that down yourself. Don't wait for them to tell you. If you do, then it has more impact. It has *less* impact if you acknowledge what they have already said. It indicates that you've been listening. It indicates that you have empathy. It indicates you understand, and people do always want to be understood.

So you come up with one or two things that have dominated the conversation. Then you don't say another word. The prospect begins to list the other things. If you've done your job, you're going to have substantially more fors than reasons against.

When you finish that, then you count. "Let's see, there's one, two, three, four, five, six, seven, eight, nine, ten reasons why you should go ahead," and you write out a 10 and circle it several times. "There are several reasons why not. There are one, two, three, four, five, six," and you make a big 6 and circle it.

Then you look directly at the prospect, lower your voice, and say, "You know, Mr. and Mrs. Prospect, if all of the people I deal with took this logical approach to making the decision such as you have, my business would be even more fun. We can have this installed within the week, or if you're really in a hurry, I'll have the serviceman out tomorrow afternoon. Which would suit your needs better?"

Let me stress a point. The prospect can come up with one reason against, and you still could miss the sale. I also want to stress that they're not going to buy for ten reasons. They're going to buy for one or two reasons. If you can give people a reason, or an excuse, for buying—like, for example, it will pay for itself, it really is more convenient for me, or whatever—your chances of making the sale are dramatically enhanced.

If they're going to decide only on one or two reasons, why do we list ten and six? Very simple. This helps to keep it sold. When they explain to their friends, relatives, and neighbors why they bought, they'll say, "Just look at all the reasons why we bought." You're giving them a logical explanation for it, and that is important.

Always remember—weave it into your presentation—that the fear of loss is greater than the desire for gain. If in your presentation, if in your close, you can make it clear that they're going to lose if they don't buy, that's more powerful than just concentrating on the gain if they do buy. The fear of loss is greater than the desire for gain.

I'll close with what I honestly believe is the most powerful single sales close I have ever heard. I'm going to modestly admit that I originated this close. I want to tell you something about the close before I share it with you. This is the close of last resort. This is when you've covered everything else.

We know 114 closes and have documented them and have written them out in *Secrets of Closing the Sale*. I said earlier, it's not how many you know, but you need to know a number of them, and you need to know them well.

One thing that used to happen to me is that when you get down to the nitty-gritty, and they have to make that decision, the prospect would say, "I just don't sign anything until I sleep on it, talk to my husband, or talk to my wife, or talk to my banker, or check with a CPA. I don't buy anything or I don't sign anything until—" and they would always bring that in the picture. They want to think about it.

You need to understand something about that. Have you ever had a prospect tell you they want to think about it? Have you ever told another salesperson you wanted to think about it? And when you told another salesperson that you wanted to think about it, did you really did think about it? You know what the basic fact is? You did that because of your soft heart and because of your compassion. You really had no intentions of buying, and you wanted to be kind to the salesperson, so you just said, "I'll let him down easy. I'll tell him I'm going to think about it." That's not being kind. That's being cruel.

In most cases, if they don't go ahead or if they give you some of these excuses and say, "I will buy later," they're trying to let you down easily. But if the sale is there, why not explore every avenue to make the sale while you're there?

With the signature close I'm going to share with you, if there is a sale there, I believe this one will get it. You don't use this to sell a small $15 or $50 order. This is something that you would use on a major purchase. Also, if you do a lot of recruiting, you can also, with adaptation, use this, and our support material shows you how. Use this as a close for recruiting.

As I give you the close, I'm going to grossly overdo it. I'm going to give you a smorgasbord of things to choose from.

You must use no more than three—probably two would be better—and your own comfort zone would dictate which ones you would use. The customer says to you, "I just don't sign anything until—" then they enumerate or give you the reason.

You start your answer with the oldest one of them all. "I know exactly how you feel, Mr. Prospect. For years and years, I felt the same way, but when I really dug into it and explored the facts, I found"—*feel, felt, found*.

Then you go into this part. "I found that everything I own or have which has any value at all, I acquired only after I had signed my name. For example, Mr. Prospect, I'm one of those extremely lucky men. I've been married for well over forty years, and I can honestly say I love my wife today infinitely more than I did the day I got her. I got her because one night, in the presence of the minister and some friends and Almighty God, I signed my name.

"I have four beautiful children. They're all mine, but before I could even take them out of the hospital, the doctor required that I sign my name. I have a beautiful home. I love that home with an absolute passion, and I got that home because one day in the presence of the builder, the savings and loan people, the insurance people, the attorney, and half the city of Dallas, I signed my name.

"I have an enormous amount of insurance, I really do. I got the insurance, and I've always had lots of insurance from the beginning. I got it because I wanted to make certain that should something happen to me that my wife would never have to go to work a day in her life if she did not want to. I wanted to ensure that my children would have a chance to get their education if they wanted it and that their standard of living would not suffer just because old Dad was not around. I got that insurance because on many different occasions, in the presence of a skilled life-insurance representative, I signed my name.

"I have a number of investments. I have them because I want to make absolutely certain that when I reach that point in life when I can no longer do what I am doing that I will not be a burden on anybody, that I can be entirely independent and self-supporting. I was able to do that because on a number of occasions, in the presence of a skilled counselor, I signed my name.

"As a matter of fact, Mr. Prospect, everything I have which has any value or significance to me at all is mine only because I signed my name. If I'm reading you right, and I believe I am, you're the kind of individual who likes not only to do things in the proper manner, and do things for his family or his business, but he likes to make progress at the same time. You can do all of those things right now by signing your name."

You say absolutely nothing else. Nothing. Now I didn't always make the sale when I did that, but I always felt good about it. Why? Because I felt that I had done everything I could in order to get the sale.

I want to stress something here. If you've been laughing and kidding and playing and backslapping all the way through the interview, and you try to use this one, I can assure you it's not going to work for you. But if it's a serious product, and you've been sincerely concerned that you buy this one, it can make a difference.

Yes, I believe skills and techniques are some of the secrets of successful selling which you must learn and relearn and update and use all of the time. Do those things, and you'll have a much richer, more exciting, and more rewarding sales career.

Selling: The Proud Profession

Zig

Many salespeople are proud of the product they sell. They're proud of the company they represent. They're proud of the income they're enjoying, and they are excited about their future, but amazingly enough, many of them are embarrassed to say, "I sell for a living."

Now you might think, "What's the big deal about that?" Let me simply say that how you feel about the sales profession plays a major role in your career. We're going to get involved now in selling you on your profession. You might say, "That sounds kind of strange, Ziglar. I've been selling twenty, thirty, forty years. You're going to sell me on being a salesperson?"

Yes, because you have an obligation that goes beyond meeting your own needs and the needs of your family. You have an obligation to the profession itself, which has been so good to you. There are lots of misconceptions about it, so let's explore it and really see what is the sales profession.

Number one, the sales profession: the very word *sell* is much better and more accurately described by the Norwegian word *selje*, which literally means *to serve*. To sell is to serve, and as you know, we've emphasized over and over that you can have everything in life you want if you will just help enough other people get what they want.

For example, I'm a prospect. You call on me selling me a product. I have a need. If you sell me something that will solve my problem, you have helped me get what I want, and obviously you got what you wanted, because you got the sale and the income along with the satisfaction that goes with it. Yes, the word *sell* really is important.

I'm convinced beyond any doubt that America is great, and one reason we're so great is the salespeople who have made it great. You can't say we're the greatest land on the face of this earth because of our size. Canada is bigger than we are. Russia is bigger than we are.

We're not the greatest because we've got the most people. India and Russia and China all have more people than we do. It's not even our natural resources, though you have to admit, we've really been tremendously blessed with natural resources. Russia has a lot of nice natural resources, as does Canada, for that matter. South America, India, China all have wonderful natural resources. That's not the reason for our greatness.

Not our technological superiority, though I'll be the first to admit that when it comes to the really great stuff that nobody is ahead of our great land. But in some areas, the Japanese are our technological masters. In others, the Germans are technological masters, the Swiss, the Swedish. We have other nations who are technologically very advanced. No, that's not the reason that we're the greatest.

I'm convinced it's because we're a land of salespeople. Let's explore that. To begin with, we were discovered by a salesman. Not by any stretch of imagination could you accuse Christopher Columbus of being a navigator. That dude was looking for India. He missed it by 12,000 miles and still went back home and told them he had found it. That is not navigation.

You might say, "OK, he wasn't a navigator, but was he a salesman?" Well, let's look at the facts. He was an Italian in Spain. That's way out of his territory. He only has one prospect, and if he doesn't make the sale, he has to swim home. Now you tell me. Was he a salesman or not?

You remember the sales call. He called on Isabella and gave her the story in a very convincing way. She listened to everything that he said, and when he had finished his sales talk, she said, "Chris, man, $12,000 for five little old ships? That price is too high." To this day a lot of people don't realize that there were five ships involved, but two of them did go over the side.

Yes, he told the story, and she heard what he said, but she didn't really hear what he was saying. So he had to really get heavy on the benefits. You see, when a salesperson sells initially, in the mind of the prospect, here's the price, and here are the benefits. That's what Isabella saw it as. Here is the price, and here are the benefits.

Chris knew he needed to sell the benefits, so he sold the fight. "We'll beat England and France and Portugal, the other powers. We'll be the first to do this. Think of the financial rewards that come our way, and if we get there first, we can spread the Word." Isabella and Ferdinand were strong Christians. "We'll be able to spread the Gospel."

He really sold the benefits, and finally the benefits had exceeded the price. Now he has a prospect. Until the benefits get higher than the price in the mind of the prospect, you don't really have a prospect. You just have a suspect.

Now he has a prospect, but the prospect has an objection. "Chris, I know it sounds like a good deal, but I don't have any money."

He took a look at her, and he said, "Look, Izzy." Now I wasn't there, so I'm not real certain this is verbatim, but he said, "You have a string of beads hanging around your neck. Let's take them down to the pawn shop and hock them. We'll finance this deal."

It wasn't quite like that, but the history book will clearly show that they did have to do some creative financing in order for them to make the trip. Then, when the trip started, you're talking about a sales job. Old Chris really had to do some selling.

You see, Columbus did not go by the charts of the day. Everybody else had been sailing due westward, and when they sailed due westward, they ran directly into those winds hitting them head-on. As a matter of fact, King John II of Portugal had just sent out another expedition trying to do the same thing, and those winds drove them backwards, but that's the way everybody went.

What Columbus did was he sailed south and then started westward ,so the prevailing winds would be behind his back. Well, old, superstitious, fearful sailors did not know what Columbus was doing. All they knew is they were going south when everybody else had always gone west, and they were concerned about it. As a matter of fact, they threatened a mutiny. They were going to throw old Columbus overboard, and Columbus had to sell. As a matter of fact, in the other two ships, which had the Pinzon brothers as their captains, one was the Niña, and one was the Pinta, the ships were ready to mutiny.

They got together for a sales meeting after a certain point, and they said, "Chris, we're fixing to get thrown overboard. Even my officers I cannot depend on. We have to put a stop to this." Columbus sold as he had never sold before in his life. He said, "Give us three more days," and just four hours before the three days expired, the call came forth.

"*Tierra. Tierra.* Land ho!" They were saved by four hours. Otherwise it'd have been back to the other side. Yes, he really had to do an awful lot of selling. He had to be very convincing. His conviction talk to them was extremely strong. Yes, Columbus discovered America because he was a supersalesperson.

Then, once that land ho! came forth, Columbus made the biggest mistake of his sales career. He did not service the account. We did not become the United States of Columbus. We became the United States of America, because another salesman entered the picture. Amerigo Vespucci came in, serviced the account, and made the sale. So we were named after a salesman, but we were also discovered by a salesman.

We were populated by a salesman. Sir Walter Raleigh toured the coffee houses of London educating and selling those ignorant, fearful, superstitious people on the idea that they should leave the security of their native land and go into the wild frontier, which was America. We were freed by salesmen.

Now let me tell you about a salesman. George Washington has to rate as one of the all-time professionals in the world of selling. Let me tell you about old George. George had to sell the merchants and the seaman and the farmers and the backwoodsmen. He had to sell all these people on going to war against the most powerful nation in the world, a nation with the largest army and the largest navy.

He had to say to them, "If we win this war, I'm awfully sorry, but I'm not going to be able to pay you.

If we lose the war, they're going to hang you to the tallest tree in town."

If you're a recruiter with your company, can you imagine having to tell a prospective salesperson, "I'm going to give you a chance, but if you make the sale, there's not going to be any money to pay you, and if you miss the sale, we're going to take you out and shoot you at sunrise." That would require some persuading.

You bet you Washington was a salesman. When we won our war, Alexander Hamilton, the Secretary of the Treasury, came to Mr. Washington and he said, "Let's persuade the Congress to appropriate some money so we can study the methods the British have used to establish their factories and agents around the world."

They appropriated the money, and they made the study. Here's what happened. The first 168 years, from 1608 to 1776, we only made it to the Appalachian Mountains, but in the next twenty-eight years, because of salespeople who set up those trading posts to supply the ever-westward trek with guns and blankets and supplies, we made it all the way to the Pacific Ocean in just twenty-eight more years.

A salesman doubled the size of our country. You think of Thomas Jefferson as a brilliant statesman. You think of him, and you think of writing the Constitution and the Bill of Rights. You think of him as the president of the United States, but he was first of all, a salesman. He sold the idea of us buying Louisiana, and that was a bunch of money involved, and a lot of people thought it was crazy, but we doubled our size with that one purchase, brought about because of a salesman.

Selling is the most secure profession we have in our country today. If my son were to come to me and say, "Dad, what would you suggest that I get into? I don't feel as secure as you do, and I want to get into something that is secure."

I would look my own son right in the eye, and I'd say, "Son, get in the profession of selling. That's where security is."

He might say, "But, Dad, doesn't everyone generally work on a commission in selling?"

I'd say, "Yes, son. Everybody in life works on a commission."

"Wait a minute. I know the president of the company and your secretary are both on salary."

"Yes, everybody down there is on salary, but they're really on commission, simply because anybody who does not produce, regardless of whether they're on salary or commission, is going to be dismissed eventually. So really all of us are on commission. You can even get to be the president of the United States, and if you don't do good, they'll get you, and you'll lose your job. Everybody in the final analysis is on a commission."

Why do I say it's so secure? Way back yonder in 1985 and 1986, there was a recession on. We know there was a recession on, because we read it in the newspapers. At our company, we decided not to join it, and I know that most of you also decided not to join it. I joined a lot of clubs, but not the recession club.

During 1985 and 1986, a lot of people lost their jobs—good people. They were honest and sincere and conscientious and hardworking and productive. It could have been the stewardess; it could have been the captain of the aircraft. It could have been the postman, or it could have been the postmaster. It could have been the schoolteacher, or it could have been the principal. It doesn't make any difference.

There were a lot of people who lost their jobs, but no honest, sincere, dedicated, hardworking salesperson lost their job. If they did, if their company went out of business, they just went down the street and got another sales job.

I will remember several years ago after another recession was on down in Atlanta. I was handling a speaking engagement, a training session. It was sales training, and just before I spoke, two fine-looking young men, they appeared to be about thirty years old, walked up to me, very well-dressed. They wanted to get their money back on their tickets.

I didn't sell the tickets. I was simply paid to speak there. I explained that to them. I said, "But why in the world would you want to miss the session?"

They said, "Well, we're salesman. We just lost our jobs."

"Both of you?"

"Yes, the boss is one of those guys. We just had a personality conflict."

"Let me ask you. Do you fellows like to sell?"

"Yes, we love to sell, and we were making good money, too."

"Would you like to have another job selling starting tomorrow?"

"Why, sure."

I said, "I can't promise you a job tomorrow, but I'll tell you what I can do. I can guarantee you twenty-five interviews during the next two weeks with people who want good salespeople, so you stick around."

They said, "OK."

I reached this point in the presentation, and I asked the audience, "How many of you are in the business of recruiting people? You give other salespeople opportunities. Could I see the hands of people in this audience who do things like that? OK. Then how many of you would like to interview two fine-looking, enthusiastic, well-trained, motivated salespeople who just had just a personality conflict, and as a result are now in the market for a sales opportunity?"

They left with over thirty business cards for interviews. You see, there's always a market for somebody who can sell, who's honest, and who's hardworking. Business handle recessions one way; us salespeople handle them in an entirely different way.

In business, a lot of times when there's a recession on, they'll call a very serious, somber, sincere meeting. "You know what the problem is. It is tough, but we're going to make it. We'll just simply turn off a few lights. We'll discharge a few people here. We'll cut all the corners. We'll suck it up and tough it out, but we're going to make it. We're going to fight this thing."

Salespeople call a meeting. The manager stands up and says, "Now, you've heard all this stuff about this recession, but we have a plan. All we have to do is just reduce our sales." Of course, it brings forth that laugh. What the sales manager does is say, "You've been hearing all that baloney about the recession. Let me tell you my response to that. We're going to put on training sessions like you've never seen before. We're going to have motivational sessions like you've never seen before. We're going to put on a contest to end all contests, and as far as the recession is going to happen, we at our company, are going to sell more and more and more."

Again, your business is not good or bad out there. It's good or bad right here, between your own two ears.

You know why I'm excited about selling? It's a democracy. I spent some time talking with a lot of salespeople. What do I like about selling? You can start real young, and you can keep at it until you're ninety-six or 106 for that matter. A man named Victor Christen, he's ninety-four years old, sells automobiles in Pasadena, California. He's excited about it. His new book is coming out on selling this year.

What I love about it, though, is the freedom. Every morning, you can get up and look in that mirror, and you can say to yourself, "You know, you're such a nice guy, or you're such a nice girl, you deserve a raise, and the board just met."

That's exciting to me. You're the chairman of the board, you're the president, you're the secretary of treasury, and yes, you also are the janitor. You're the one who decides whether to give yourself a raise or even to lay yourself off, whether to move yourself up or bring yourself down by your decisions and your actions, not subjected to whims of others.

As salespeople, we're in business *for* ourselves, but not *by* ourselves. Minimal capital investments involved. There's no discrimination in the world of selling. It is probably the closest thing to a pure democracy that I have ever seen. We don't care what your race or your sex or your creed or your color might be. Your opportunity is the same, and it is unlimited.

Three of the most successful salespeople I know finished the third grade (in two cases) or the eighth grade, but by hard work and diligence, they've applied themselves and their skills, learned the procedures and techniques, and they've been enormously successful.

Did you know that 37 percent of the country's fastest-growing companies have chief executive officers who came up from the sales world? Selling is fun, and it's challenging, and it's rewarding, and as Red Motley said so eloquently, "Nothing happens until somebody sells something."

Have you ever thought this one through? What happens when you make a sale? A lot of salespeople don't know what does happen when you make a sale. Let's trace it.

First of all, you understand you write that sale on an order pad. Did you ever stop to realize that order pad didn't start out as an order pad? It started out as a tree. You're the person who paid those people who went out in the woods and cut that tree down when you got out there and made that sale. A bunch of people had to take that tree and haul it to the paper mill, and you're the person who paid those people to haul that tree from the forest down to the paper mill. In the paper mill, hundreds of people are involved in manufacturing that tree into paper. You're the person who paid those people to manufacture that tree into paper when you got out there and made the sale.

It goes a lot further than that. You take part of your profits. When you make a sale, you do make a profit. Your manager makes a profit, and if you're lucky, your company makes a profit. If the company doesn't make a profit, you're soon not going to have a job with that company. They're going to be out of business.

But you take part of your profit. You go down to the grocery store and buy a can of beans. When you buy that can of beans, the grocer says, "If you're going to buy my beans, I have to get some more." So he goes to the wholesaler and says, "I need more beans." The wholesaler says, "If you're going to buy my beans, I have to get some more." He goes to the cannery and says, "Need more beans."

The cannery says, "If you're going to buy my beans, I need to get some more." He goes to the farmer and says, "Need more beans." The farmer says, "If you're going to buy my beans, I have to raise some more. To do that, I need to get a new tractor, because the one I have is worn out."

The farmer goes down to the dealer and says, "Hey, I have to have a new tractor." The dealer says, "If you're going to buy my new tractor, I have to get another one, because this is the last one we have in inventory." He goes to the factory and says, "Hey, I need a new tractor." The factory says, "If you're going to buy my tractors, I have to manufacture some more, and to do that, we have to bring in iron, copper, plastic, steel, aluminum, lead, zinc, spark plugs. We're going to set up factories all over the world to manufacture those things."

And all of that happened because one day you got out there and made a sale.

That's what you ought to tell folks. Regardless of what that other person does, regardless of their status and their rank in life, that person is enjoying the standard of living they are because you and others like you are out there in the world selling.

Then why is it that in the sales profession, we do not enjoy the reputation that we should? Why do some people look down on us?

I think one basic problem is that we've sold our goods, we've sold our services, we've sold our companies, but we've not sold our profession. You know the American Medical Association spends tons of money and have their own publicity agents selling what they do. The same is true for the bankers' association, the dental association, and so many others. We need an American Sales Association, where we sell the profession of selling.

Why, even the dictionary is all fouled up. Did you know that the dictionary says the word *sell* means *to deliver up, to make a bribe for, to betray, to fool a person,* a deception, a hoax? When those dirty dogs write stuff like that, that gets my dander up, because there's not a word of truth in it. We ought to get after them to take it out of there and identify it for what it is.

One problem too is we still have that old Yankee peddler concept. A lot of people think that selling is making people want something they don't need or which they have no real use for or which simply has no value. Or they think selling is making people buy something they don't even want.

Then Broadway does its part. They have a play called *The Music Man,* and Harold Hill, the consummate con man in River City, Iowa, does a number on us, and we get an impression.

But the worst thing I ever saw in my life—I couldn't believe the vulgarity and the obscenity of it. I don't mean it was pornographic as far as the pictures and the words were concerned, but they way they describe and picture the salesman is absolutely vulgar, unseemly, pornographic, and untrue. Willy Loman in *Death of a Salesman* has no more relationship to what we as salespeople are like and what we do and the role we play than the man in the moon.

They showed that thing on Broadway forever. Then the rascals put it on television not once, not twice, but three times. It finally died like it ought to, I thought. Then would you believe that they revived it? They revived it, and they showed it another long time there on Broadway, and then they put it back on television.

How ridiculous can we get? What is the real truth? I'll tell you the role we play and why it's so important. The Secretary of Commerce of the United States, a man who ought to know, said this: "We need one million more professional salespeople." Why? Because every time you make that sale, industry turns, and business comes there.

What can we do? We need to spread that word. We need to support confidence-building organizations like the sales and marketing clubs, the swap clubs, Salesman with a Purpose, or the National Speakers Association. They in reality are for speakers, but because so many of them are outstanding sales trainers, and everybody is a salesperson, we need to get involved in organizations like that.

Here's something we really need to do a lot of thinking on. We need to let people know what the salesperson and the sales profession is all about.

Many years ago, this was written, and I share it with you.

I'm a salesman. I'm proud to be in sales because more than anyone else, I, and millions of others like me, built America.

The man who builds a better mousetrap or a better anything would starve to death if he waited for people to beat a pathway to his door. Regardless of how good or how needed the product or service might be, it has to be sold.

Eli Whitney was laughed at when he showed his cotton gin. Edison had to install his electric light free of charge in an office building before anyone would even look at it. The first sewing machine was smashed to pieces by a Boston mob. People scoffed at the idea of railroads. They thought that traveling even thirty miles an hour would stop the circulation of the blood. McCormick strived for fourteen years to get people to use his reaper. Westinghouse was considered a fool for stating that he could stop a train with wind. Morse had to plead before ten Congresses before they would even look at his telegraph.

The public didn't go around demanding these things. They had to be sold!!

They needed thousands of salesman, trailblazers, pioneers, people who could persuade with the same effectiveness as the inventor could invent. Salesmen took these inventions, sold the public on what these products could do, taught customers how to use them, and then taught businessmen how to make a profit from them.

As a salesman, I've done more to make America what it is today than any other person you know. I was just as vital in your great-great-grandfather's day as I am in yours, and I'll be just as vital in your great-great-grandson's day.

I have educated more people, created more jobs, taken more drudgery from the laborer's work, given more people a fuller and richer life than anyone in history. I've dragged prices down, pushed quality up, and made it possible for you to enjoy the comforts and luxuries of automobiles, radios, electric refrigerators, televisions, and air-conditioned homes and buildings.

I've healed the sick, given security to the aged, and put thousands of young men and women through college. I've made it possible for inventors to invent, for factories to hum, and for ships to sale the seven seas. How much money you find in your pay envelope next week and whether in the future you will enjoy the luxuries of prefabricated homes, stratospheric flying airplanes, and a new world of jet propulsion, and atomic power depends on me.

The loaf of bread that you bought today was on a baker's shelf because I made sure that a farmer's wheat got to the mill, that the mill made the wheat into flour, and that the flour was delivered to your baker. Without me, the wheels of industry would come to a grinding halt, and with that jobs, marriages, politics, and freedom of thought would be a thing of the past. I AM A SALESMAN and I'm both proud and grateful that as such I serve my family, my fellow man, and my country.

Yes, I am a salesman. Be proud that you sell, and as my friend from down under, Mr. John Nevin, says, "If somebody says, 'Here comes a salesman,' don't let him down."

Buy these ideas, follow through on the procedures and the techniques and the skills we've been sharing with you. I'll close by saying I'll see you, and yes, I do mean *you*, at the top in the world of selling.

Index